Key Stage 2 Maths Practice Papers
Contents, Instructions and Answers

Author: Faisal Nasim

Contents

Introduction

This practice resource consists of two complete sets of Key Stage 2 maths practice test papers. Each set contains similar test papers to those that pupils will take at the end of Year 6. They can be used any time throughout the year to provide practice for the Key Stage 2 tests.

The result of the papers will provide a good idea of pupils' strengths and weaknesses.

Administering the Tests

- Children should work in a quiet environment where they can complete each test undisturbed.
- Children should have a pen or pencil, ruler, eraser and protractor. A calculator is not allowed.
- Handwriting is not assessed but children should write their answers clearly.
- The amount of time allowed per test varies, so children should check the time given on each test paper.

Marking the Tests

Each set of maths practice papers is worth a total of 110 marks:
- Paper 1: arithmetic is worth 40 marks
- Paper 2: reasoning is worth 35 marks
- Paper 3: reasoning is worth 35 marks

Use this answer booklet to mark the test papers and add up the total marks for Paper 1, Paper 2 and Paper 3. As a general guideline, if a child gets 61 or more marks across the three papers (i.e. 61 or more out of 110), they are reaching the expected standard. Keep in mind that the exact number of marks required to achieve the expected standard may vary year by year depending on the overall difficulty of the test.

Answers

Content domain coverage for the questions in this paper are shown in the tables of answers below. Information about these codes can be found in the KS2 Maths test framework.

Set A Paper 1: arithmetic

Question (Content domain)		Requirement	Mark
1	(4N2b)	3,023	1
2	(4C2)	3,203	1
3	(4F4)	$1\frac{3}{8}$ OR $\frac{11}{8}$ Accept equivalent mixed numbers, fractions or exact decimal equivalent, e.g. 1.375 Do not accept rounded or truncated decimals.	1
4	(4C6b)	345	1
5	(3C1)	385	1
6	(5F8)	9.523	1
7	(4C6b)	240	1
8	(3C7)	182	1
9	(4C6a)	7	1
10	(4C7)	705	1
11	(4C2)	3,166	1
12	(4C6b)	800	1
13	(6N3)	600,000	1
14	(6C9)	78	1
15	(6F5a)	$\frac{1}{7}$ Accept equivalent fraction, e.g. $\frac{6}{42}$ or **exact** decimal equivalent, e.g. 0.14	1
16	(5C6a)	3,000	1
17	(5C7b)	59	1
18	(6F9a)	0.008	1
19	(5C6b)	3,465,000	1
20	(6C7b)	Award **TWO** marks for answer of 32 Working must be carried through to a final answer for **ONE** mark. Award **ONE** mark for a formal method of division with no more than **ONE** arithmetic error.	Up to 2
21	(4F8)	5.36	1
22	(6C7a)	Award **TWO** marks for answer of 193,500 Award **ONE** mark for a formal method of long multiplication with no more than **ONE** arithmetic error. Working must be carried through to a final answer for **ONE** mark. **Do not** award any marks if the error is in the place value, e.g. the omission of the zero when multiplying by tens.	Up to 2
23	(5F4)	$\frac{1}{10}$ Accept equivalent fractions or an **exact** decimal equivalent, e.g. 0.1	1
24	(6C7a)	Award **TWO** marks for answer of 32,674 Award **ONE** mark for a formal method of long multiplication with no more than **ONE** arithmetic error. Working must be carried through to a final answer for **ONE** mark. **Do not** award any marks if the error is in the place value, e.g. the omission of the zero when multiplying by tens.	Up to 2
25	(5F8)	22.161	1
26	(6F4)	$\frac{3}{5}$ Accept equivalent fraction, or **exact** decimal equivalent, e.g. 0.6	1
27	(6F5b)	$\frac{1}{8}$ Accept equivalent fraction, e.g. $\frac{3}{24}$ or **exact** decimal equivalent, e.g. 0.125	1
28	(6F5b)	$\frac{5}{12}$ Accept equivalent fractions or **exact** decimal equivalent, e.g. 0.416	1
29	(6R2)	182 Do not accept 182%	1
30	(6F4)	$4\frac{1}{10}$ OR $\frac{41}{10}$ Accept equivalent mixed numbers, fractions or **exact** decimal equivalent, e.g. 4.1 Do not accept rounded or truncated decimals. Do not accept $3\frac{11}{10}$	1
31	(6R2)	56 Do not accept 56%	1
32	(6C9, 5C5d)	$5\frac{7}{24}$	1
33	(6F9b)	180	1
34	(6R2)	240 Do not accept 240%	1
35	(5F5)	$94\frac{1}{2}$ Accept equivalent fractions or **exact** decimal equivalent, e.g. 94.5 or $\frac{189}{2}$	1
36	(6C7b)	Award **TWO** marks for answer of 39 Working must be carried through to a final answer for **ONE** mark. Award **ONE** mark for a formal method of division with no more than **ONE** arithmetic error.	Up to 2

Set A, Paper 2: reasoning

Question (Content domain)		Requirement	Mark	Additional guidance
1	(4S2)	190 10	1 1	
2	(4C6a)	Three boxes completed correctly as shown: | x	9	5
8	72	40
12	108	60		1	
3	(5C6b)	The correct number circled as shown: (4030)	1	Accept alternative unambiguous indications, e.g. number ticked.
4	(4C4) (4S2)	Award **TWO** marks for answer of 3,148 Award **ONE** mark for evidence of an appropriate method, e.g. • 2,693 + 1,012 = 3,705; 6,853 − 3,705	Up to 2	Answer need not be obtained for the award of **ONE** mark.
5	(4M4c)	Award **TWO** marks for an answer of 2:17 P.M. Accept 14:17 Award **ONE** mark for evidence of an appropriate method, e.g. • $2\frac{1}{4}$ hours = 2 hours 15 minutes 2 hours 15 minutes + 22 minutes = 2 hours 37 minutes 11:40 + 2 hours 37 minutes = • Sight of a number line showing 11:40 + steps for 37 minutes and $2\frac{1}{4}$ hours.	Up to 2	
6	(4N2b) (4N2b)	1,026 tickets 16,269 tickets	1 1	
7	(5C4)	Award **TWO** marks for answer of 2,884 Award **ONE** mark for evidence of an appropriate method, e.g. • 1,576 + 9,854 = 11,430; 11,430 − 8,546	Up to 2	Answer need not be obtained for the award of **ONE** mark.
8	(4F2)		1	Accept alternative unambiguous indications, e.g. shapes circled.
9	(6A2)	110 3	1 1	The answer is a time interval. Accept 1 hour 50 minutes.
10	(4F6a, 4F6b)	0.2 and $\frac{4}{20}$ ticked, Both answers indicated for the award of 1 mark	Up to 2	Award **ONE** mark for each correct answer. If two answers are correct and one incorrect, award **ONE** mark. If one answer is correct and one is incorrect, award **NO** marks.
11	(6G2b)	Award **TWO** marks for triangular prism and cube ticked. Award **ONE** mark for: • the cube and prism ticked and not more than one incorrect shape ticked OR • only one correct shape ticked and no incorrect shape ticked.	Up to 2	Accept alternative unambiguous indications, e.g. shapes circled.
12	(5F8)	0.428 0.72 2.134 2.5	1	
13	(5M9a)	Award **TWO** marks for answer of 91p Award **ONE** mark for evidence of an appropriate method, e.g. • 12 × 95p = £11.40; £11.40 − £10.49	Up to 2	Award **ONE** mark for answer of £91 OR £91p as evidence of an appropriate method. Answer need not be obtained for the award of **ONE** mark.
14	(5N3b)	2012	1	Do not accept answer in words.
15	(6R4)	20	1	Accept 20:15 OR 15:20
16	(5G4b)		1	
17	(6C8) (5M9a)	Award **TWO** marks for answer of £1.73 Award **ONE** mark for evidence of an appropriate method, e.g. • 20 − 14.81 = 5.19; 5.19 ÷ 3	Up to 2	Award **ONE** mark for answer of £173 OR £173p as evidence of an appropriate method. Answer need not be obtained for the award of **ONE** mark.
18	(6R2)	15	1	

19	(6P3)	Quadrilateral completed as shown:	1	Accept very slight inaccuracies in drawing, within a 2 mm radius of the correct point.
20	(6N2)	An explanation showing 4,052,234 is greater than 967,358 or that 967,358 is less than 4,052,234, e.g. • 4,052,234 has four million and 967,358 is less than 1 million • 4,052,234 is more than a million, but 967,358 is not • 967,358 doesn't have any millions, but 4,052,234 has 4	1	
21	(5M9b) (6R3)	Award **TWO** marks for answer of 15.5 Award **ONE** mark for evidence of an appropriate method, e.g. • $775 \div 50$ OR • 100 km is 2 cm; 50 km is 1 cm 500 km is 10 cm; 25 km is 0.5 cm 10 cm + 2 cm + 2 cm + 1 cm + 0.5 cm	Up to 2	Answer need not be obtained for the award of **ONE** mark. Do not accept incorrect proportions in any step without evidence of the calculation performed.
22	(6F4)	Award **TWO** marks for answer of $\frac{5}{8}$ Award **ONE** mark for evidence of an appropriate method, e.g. • $\frac{1}{4} + \frac{1}{8} =$ • $\frac{2}{8} + \frac{1}{8} = \frac{3}{8}$ • $1 - \frac{3}{8}$ • $\frac{1}{4} + \frac{1}{8} + \frac{1}{8} + \frac{1}{8}$	Up to 2	Accept equivalent fractions or exact decimal equivalent, e.g. 0.625 Answer need not be obtained for the award of **ONE** mark.
23	(6R3)	1:3	1	Accept other equivalent ratios, e.g. 3:9 Do not accept reversed ratios, e.g. 9:3

Set A, Paper 3: reasoning

Question (Content domain)	Requirement	Mark	Additional guidance
1 (5N2)	Award **ONE** mark for: E, B, C, A, D	1	Accept: £87,500 B £140,500 £147,250 £151,600
2 (3N2a)	698 771	1 1	

3 (3C2)	Award **TWO** marks for:
	  2 7 **4**
	+5 **5** 2
	  8 2 6
	Award **ONE** mark for two digits correct.
		Up to 2	

4 (5C5c)	Award **TWO** marks for all placed as shown: Award **ONE** mark for three numbers placed correctly.	Up to 2	Accept alternative unambiguous indications, e.g. lines drawn from the numbers to the appropriate regions of the diagram. Do not accept numbers written in more than one region.
5 (3C8, 3C6)	Award **TWO** marks for answer of 330 (pens). Award **ONE** mark for evidence of an appropriate method, e.g. $(60 \times 4) + (30 \times 3) = 330$; $60 \times 5.5 = 330$	Up to 2	

6	(4G2c)	Diagram completed correctly as shown: Mirror line	1	Accept inaccurate drawing within a radius of 2 mm of the correct point, provided the intention is clear. Diagram need not be shaded. Diagram need not include edges drawn along the gridlines.
7	(6F2)	$\dfrac{4}{5} = \dfrac{8}{10} = \dfrac{16}{20}$	1 1	
8	(5F10)	Numbers circled: 0.07 0.3	1	Accept alternative unambiguous indications, e.g. numbers ticked or underlined.
9	(5M9a)	Award **TWO** marks for answer of 37p Award **ONE** mark for evidence of an appropriate method, e.g. $190 \div 2 = 95$; $132 - 95$ OR $190 \div 10 = 19$; $5 \times 19 = 95$; $132 - 95$	Up to 2	Answer need not be obtained for the award of **ONE** mark. Award **ONE** mark for answer of 0.37p OR £37p OR £37 as evidence of an appropriate method.
10	(3F2)	Award **TWO** marks for all shading as shown: Any four squares of the oblong, any eight segments of the circle and any two sections of the parallelogram. Award **ONE** mark for two diagrams correct.	Up to 2	Accept alternative unambiguous indications of parts shaded.
11	(5M9c)	Award **TWO** marks for answer of 50 Award **ONE** mark for evidence of an appropriate method, e.g. • 1.5 kg = 1,500 g; $1,500 \div 30$	Up to 2	Answer need not be obtained for **ONE** mark. Units must be converted correctly for **ONE** mark.
12	(6A2)	76 30	1 1	
13	(5F5)	Award **TWO** marks for a correct answer of 360.75 (kg) Award **ONE** mark for evidence of an appropriate method, e.g. • $27\frac{3}{4} \times 13 =$ • $(27 \times 13) + (\frac{3}{4} \times 13) =$ • $27.75 \times 13 =$ • $\frac{111}{4} \times 13 =$	Up to 2	Answer need not be obtained for the award of **ONE** mark.
14	(6C5)	18 AND 36 only	1	Numbers may be given in either order.
15	(5M5)	Award **TWO** marks for answer of 95°F Award **ONE** mark for evidence of an appropriate method, e.g. • $104 - 86 = 18$; $18 \div 2 = 9$; $9 + 86$ OR • $104 - 86 = 18$; $18 \div 2 = 9$; $104 - 9$ OR • $104 + 86 = 190$; $190 \div 2$	Up to 2	Answer need not be obtained for the award of **ONE** mark.
16	(6G4b) (6G4a)	$a = 40$ $b = 70$	1 1	If the answers to a and b are incorrect, award **ONE** mark if $a + b = 110°$
17	(6N2)	8,999,990	1	
18	(6C8)	200 (cans)	1	
19	(6C8)	Award **THREE** marks for answer of £127.20 Award **TWO** marks for: • sight of £102 AND £10.20 AND £15.00 as all multiplication steps completed correctly OR • sight of 10,200p AND 1,020p AND 1,500p as all multiplication steps completed correctly. • evidence of an appropriate complete method with no more than one arithmetic error. Award **ONE** mark for evidence of an appropriate complete method.	Up to 3	Answer need not be obtained for the award of **ONE** mark. No marks are awarded if there is more than one misread or if the maths is simplified. Award **TWO** marks if an appropriate complete method with the misread number is followed through correctly. Award **ONE** mark for all multiplication steps completed correctly with the misread number OR evidence of an appropriate complete method with the misread number followed through correctly with no more than one arithmetic error.
20	(6P2)	(–15, –20)	1	
21	(6A2)	▮ = 4 ● = 3	1	

Set B, Paper 1: arithmetic

Question (Content domain)	Requirement	Mark
1 (3N2b)	1,053	1
2 (3C2)	442	1
3 (4C6b)	11,500	1
4 (3C1)	568	1
5 (3C2)	1,219	1
6 (3C7)	14	1
7 (4C6b)	280	1
8 (3C1)	609	1
9 (3C7)	31	1
10 (4C7)	2,268	1
11 (3C7)	558	1
12 (5C6a)	3,200	1
13 (5F5)	800	1
14 (5F8)	8.349	1
15 (5C7b)	175	1
16 (5F8)	44.398	1
17 (5F8)	188.97	1
18 (5C2)	230,329	1
19 (6C9)	36	1
20 (6F9a)	0.03	1
21 (4F8)	3.75	1
22 (4C6b)	110	1
23 (5C7a)	Award **TWO** marks for answer of 14,097. Award **ONE** mark for a formal method of long multiplication with no more than **ONE** arithmetic error. Working must be carried through to a final answer for **ONE** mark. **Do not** award any marks if the error is in the place value, e.g. the omission of the zero when multiplying by tens.	Up to 2
24 (4F4)	$1\frac{2}{9}$ or $\frac{11}{9}$ Accept equivalent fractions or **exact** decimal equivalent, e.g. 1.222 Do not accept rounded or truncated decimals.	1
25 (6R2)	810 Do not accept 810%	1
26 (6F9b)	64.5	1
27 (5F4)	$\frac{1}{3}$ Accept equivalent fractions or **exact** decimal equivalent, e.g. 0.333'.	1
28 (6C7b)	Award **TWO** marks for answer of 26 Working must be carried through to a final answer for **ONE** mark. Award **ONE** mark for a formal method of division with no more than **ONE** arithmetic error.	Up to 2
29 (6R2)	93	1
30 (6C7a)	Award **TWO** marks for answer of 313,698 Working must be carried through to a final answer for **ONE** mark. Award **ONE** mark for a formal method of long multiplication with no more than **ONE** arithmetic error. **Do not** award any marks if the error is in the place value, e.g. the omission of the zero when multiplying by tens.	Up to 2
31 (6F4)	$1\frac{11}{20}$ or $\frac{31}{20}$ Accept equivalent mixed numbers, fractions or **exact** decimal equivalent, e.g. 1.55 Do not accept rounded or truncated decimals.	1
32 (6C7b)	Award **TWO** marks for answer of 51 Working must be carried through to a final answer for **ONE** mark. Award **ONE** mark for a formal method of division with no more than **ONE** arithmetic error.	Up to 2
33 (6F5b)	$\frac{1}{7}$ Accept equivalent fractions or **exact** decimal equivalent, e.g. 0.142	1
34 (5F5)	36	1
35 (6C9, 5C5d)	$1\frac{7}{12}$	1
36 (6C9)	88	1

Set B, Paper 2: reasoning

Question (Content domain)	Requirement	Mark	Additional guidance
1 (4M4b)	Both clocks ticked: 07:50 and 19:50	1	Accept alternative unambiguous indications, e.g. circled.
2 (3C3, 3C2)	92 − 28 = 64 or 92 − 64 = 28 and 85 − 47 = 38	1 1	
3 (3C1)	Award **TWO** marks for numbers in order as shown: **61** 77 93 **109** 125 141 **157** Award **ONE** mark for two numbers correct.	Up to 2	
4 (6A2)	△ = 31 ☆ = 24	1 1	If the answers to △ and ☆ are incorrect, award **ONE** mark if △ + ☆ = 55
5 (5F8)	0.079 0.509 0.89 3.001 4.8	1	
6 (4F10b)	Award **TWO** marks for answer of 1.70 Award **ONE** mark for evidence of an appropriate method, e.g. • 2.45 + 1.85 = 4.30; 6 − 4.30 • 6 − 2.45 = 3.55; 3.55 − 1.85	Up to 2	Award **ONE** mark for answer of 170 metres as evidence of an appropriate method. Answer need not be obtained for the award of **ONE** mark.

7	(4G4)	A and F	1	Letters may be in either order.
		B, D and E	1	Letters may be in any order.

8	(6C8)	Award **TWO** marks for answer of 42p OR £0.42
		Award **ONE** mark for evidence of an appropriate method, e.g.
		• 50p + 20p + 2p + 2p = 74p
		   £2.00 – 74p = £1.26
		   £1.26 ÷ 3
			Up to 2	Award **ONE** mark for answer of £42 OR £42p OR 0.42p as evidence of an appropriate method.
				Answer need not be obtained for the award of **ONE** mark.

9	(5S1)	47	1	The answer is a time interval.
		10:45	1	The answer is a specific time.
10	(6C7a)	Award **TWO** marks for answer of 4,800 Award **ONE** mark for evidence of an appropriate method with no more than one arithmetic error.	Up to 2	Misreads are not allowed.
11	(5M8)	B	1	Accept 40
12	(4P2)	The triangle has moved 6 squares to the right and 3 squares down.	1	
13	(4M4c)	480	1	
		7,200	1	
14	(3C4)	Award **TWO** marks for answer of 24 Award **ONE** mark for evidence of an appropriate method, e.g. • 3.5 × 4 = 14; 14 – 8 = 6; 6 × 4	Up to 2	Answer need not be obtained for the award of **ONE** mark.
15	(5N4)	The factory fills 50,000 boxes with 40 cans a day. ✓	1	Accept alternative unambiguous indications, e.g. underlined.
16	(5N4)	Award **TWO** marks for: 40,900; 4,100; 400 Award **ONE** mark for two boxes correct.	Up to 2	
17	(5M9c)	Award **TWO** marks for answer of 1.8 Award **ONE** mark for evidence of an appropriate method, e.g. • 1.5 × 12 = 18; 18 ÷ 10	Up to 2	Answer need not be obtained for the award of **ONE** mark.
18	(5M4)	35 min 2 sec	1	
		29 min 24 sec	1	
19	(6G2a)	E	1	
20	(5F10)	Award **TWO** marks for answer of £12.90 Award **ONE** mark for evidence of an appropriate method, e.g. • £1.75 + £2.55 = £4.30; £4.30 × 3	Up to 2	Award **ONE** mark for answer of £1,290 OR £1,290p OR £12.9 as evidence of an appropriate method. Answer need not be obtained for the award of **ONE** mark.
21	(6C8)	An explanation that shows that 6,832 can be made by adding 427 to 16 × 427, e.g. • '6,832 + 427 = 17 × 427' • '17 × 427 is 427 more than 6,832' • 'Because this is the same as 16 × 427 = 6,832 so add one more 326 to get the answer' • 'You add 427 to 6,832 and your answer will be correct' • 'Because you can add 427 to the answer of 16 × 427' • '6,832 + 427'.	1	Do not accept explanation that simply calculates 427 × 17 = 7,259 Do not accept vague or incorrect explanations, e.g. • 'You could add another 427' • 'The difference between 16 and 17 is 1 so you add 427 and that is one more'.

Set B, Paper 3: reasoning

Question (Content domain)		Requirement	Mark	Additional guidance
1	(5C6b)	100	1	
2	(4C8)	74 × 5	1	
3	(3C8)	6	1	
4	(6N5/ 6S1)	10	1	Do not accept –10 or 10–
		–4	1	Do not accept 4–
5	(5S1) (4M4b)	The correct time circled: 14:25	1	Accept alternative unambiguous indications, e.g. 14:25 ticked. Accept 15:47 circled as well as 14:25, provided no other is circled.
6	(4F10b)	221.19	1	
7	(6P2)	Triangle with vertices at (1,3) AND (4,3) AND (1,6) drawn as shown: 	1	Accept very slight inaccuracies in drawing.

8	(6C5)	Award **TWO** marks for any three of the following numbers written in any order: 5, 10, 20, 40 Award **ONE** mark for two numbers correct.	Up to 2	
9	(5S1) (4S2)	6	1	Do not accept 360 minutes.
10	(6G5)	16	1	
11	(4M5)	518(ml) or 0.518(l)	1	Do not accept incorrect units.
12	(6G2a) (4G4)	Circled correctly:	1	Accept alternative unambiguous indications, e.g. ticked.
13	(4C8)	An explanation that shows Clara has four times as many biscuits as Harry, e.g. • 32 × 4 is 4 times as many as 16 × 2 • 128 is four times 32 • 128 ÷ 4 = 32 • 128 ÷ 32 = 4 • 32 × 4 = 128 • Clara buys twice as many packets of twice as many biscuits, so it's doubled twice • 32 is double 16 and 4 is double 2, so it's doubled twice • Harry buys half the amount of biscuits and each packet has half the number of biscuits, so he has $\frac{1}{4}$ of the amount.	1	Do not accept vague or incomplete explanations, e.g. • Clara buys more packets and there are more biscuits in each packet • Clara buys twice as many packets of twice as many biscuits • 32 is double 16 and 4 is double 2.
14	(6R1) (5M9a)	Award **TWO** marks for answer of £1.32 Award **ONE** mark for evidence of an appropriate method, e.g. • £1.65 × 4 = £6.60; £6.60 ÷ 5	Up to 2	Award **ONE** mark for answer of £132p OR 13.2p as evidence of an appropriate method. Answer need not be obtained for the award of **ONE** mark.
15	(5C8b)	Award **TWO** marks for answer of 1,250 Award **ONE** mark for evidence of an appropriate method, e.g. • 350 × 2 = 700; 3,200 – 700 = 2,500; 2,500 ÷ 2	Up to 2	Answer need not be obtained for the award of **ONE** mark.
16	(3G2)	**H** is circled.	1	Accept alternative unambiguous indications, e.g. letter ticked.
17	(6R2)	360	1	
18	(6R3)	20	1	
19	(6C3)	5 + 3 + 3 ✓	1	Accept alternative unambiguous indications, e.g. underlined.
20	(5M7b) (5C7a)	Award **THREE** marks for answer of 18 Award **TWO** marks for: • 918 as evidence of 34 × 27 completed correctly **OR** • evidence of an appropriate method with no more than one arithmetic error. Award **ONE** mark for evidence of an appropriate method.	Up to 3	Answer need not be obtained for the award of **ONE** mark. A misread of a number may affect the award of marks. Award **TWO** marks for an appropriate method using the misread number followed through correctly to a final answer.
21	(4N6)	Award **TWO** marks for 11 AND 12 Award **ONE** mark for: • only one correct number and no incorrect number **OR** • 11 AND 12 AND not more than one incorrect number.	Up to 2	Award **ONE** mark for answer of 66 AND 72 AND no more than one incorrect number.
22	(6F4/6A3)	$\frac{1}{4}$ written in the first box $3\frac{1}{4}$ or $\frac{13}{4}$ written in the last box	1 1	Accept equivalent fractions or **exact** decimal equivalent, e.g. 0.25 Accept equivalent fractions or **exact** decimal equivalent, e.g. 3.25

23	(6A1)	Award **TWO** marks for answer of 19
		
		Award **ONE** mark for evidence of an appropriate method, e.g.
		• 15 + 4 + 2 widths = 38 + 1 width
		  19 + 2 widths = 38 + 1 width
		  19 + 1 width = 38; 38 – 19
			Up to 2	Answer need not be obtained for the award of **ONE** mark.
				Award **ONE** mark for a method which uses algebraic representation correctly.

24	(6M8b) (6R1)	Award **TWO** marks for answer of 32 Award **ONE** mark for evidence of an appropriate method, e.g. • 8 × 8 × 8 = 512; 512 ÷ 8 = 64; 64 ÷ 2	Up to 2	Answer need not be obtained for the award of **ONE** mark.
25	(6A4)	Both numbers correct as shown: b = 4 × a – 2	1	

Key Stage 2

Mathematics
Set A

Paper 1: arithmetic

Name						
School						
Date of Birth	Day		Month		Year	

Instructions

Do not use a calculator to answer the questions in this test.

Questions and answers

You have **30 minutes** to complete this test.

Write your answer in the box provided for each question.

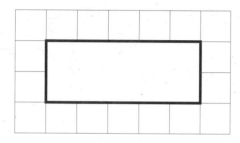

You should give all answers as a single value.

For questions expressed as mixed numbers or common fractions, you should give your answers as mixed numbers or common fractions.

If you cannot do a question, move on to the next one, then go back to it at the end if you have time.

If you finish before the end of the test, go back and check your answers.

Marks

The numbers under the boxes at the side of the page tell you the number of marks for each question.

Answers are worth one or two marks.

Long division and long multiplication questions are worth **TWO marks each**. You will get TWO marks for a correct answer; you may get **ONE mark** for showing a correct method.

1   23 + 3,000 =

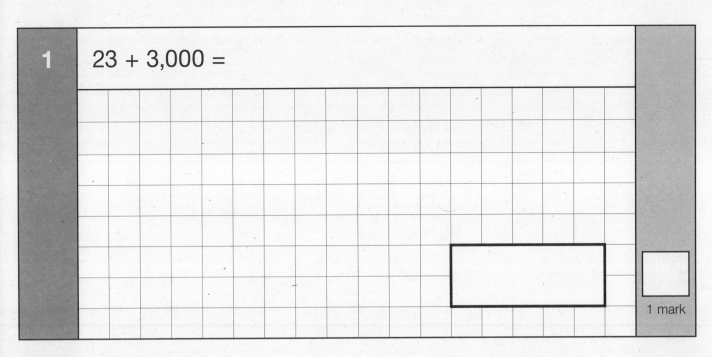

1 mark

2   657 + 2,546 =

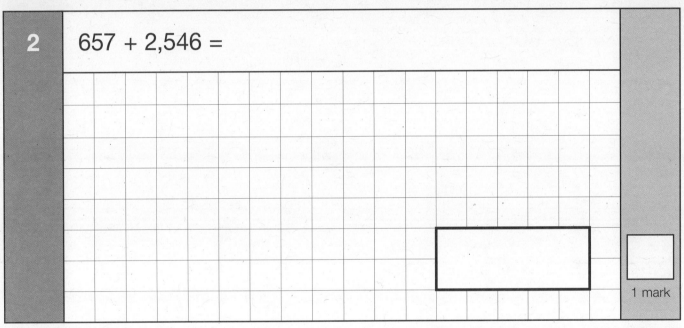

1 mark

3 $\dfrac{4}{8} + \dfrac{7}{8} =$

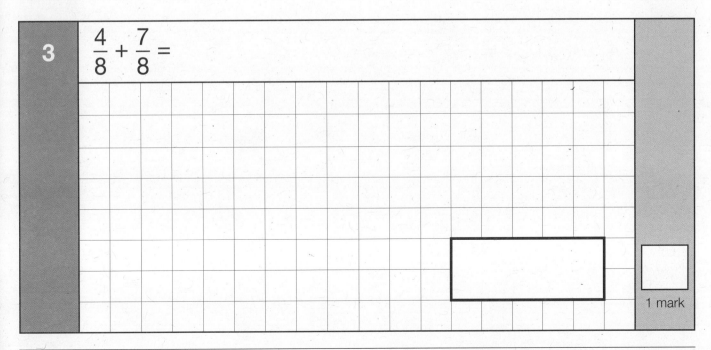

1 mark

4 $345 \div 1 =$

1 mark

5 $465 - 80 =$

1 mark

6 $4.5 + 5.023 =$

1 mark

7 $8 \times 3 \times 10 =$

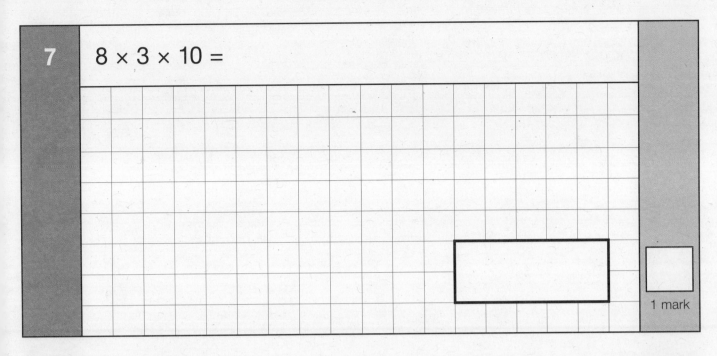

1 mark

8 $7 \times 26 =$

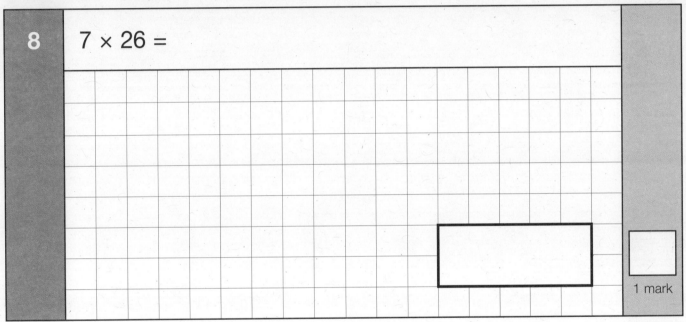

1 mark

9 $84 \div 12 =$

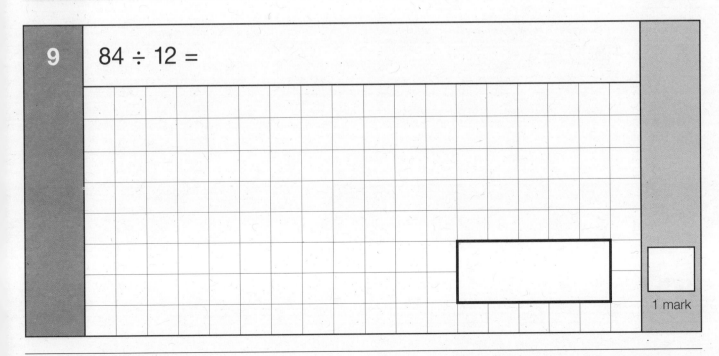

1 mark

10 $235 \times 3 =$

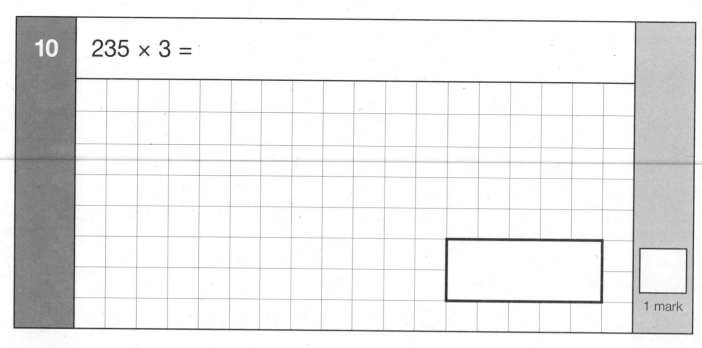

1 mark

11 $3{,}813 - 647 =$

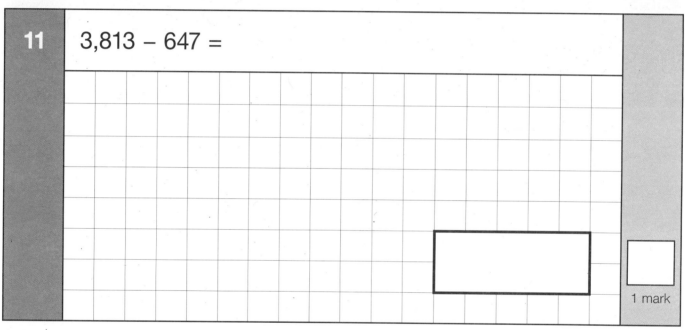

1 mark

12 $4{,}800 \div 6 =$

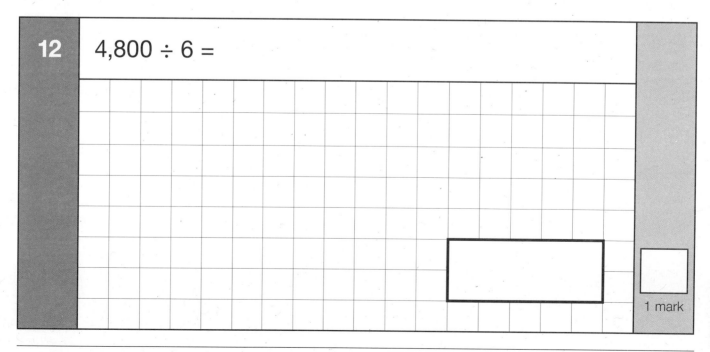

1 mark

13 4,600,800 = 4,000,000 + ⬚ + 800

14 72 + (48 ÷ 8) =

15 $\dfrac{2}{7} \times \dfrac{3}{6} =$

16 50 × 60 =

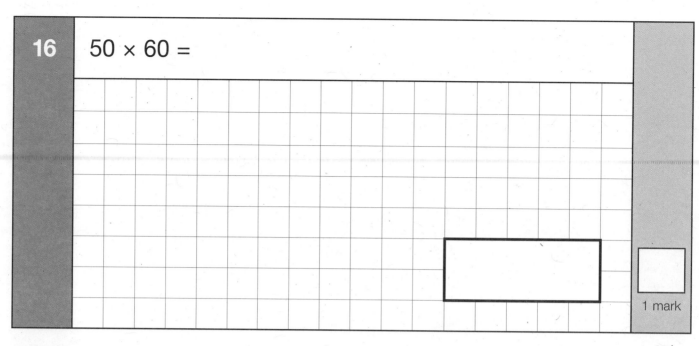

1 mark

17 472 ÷ 8 =

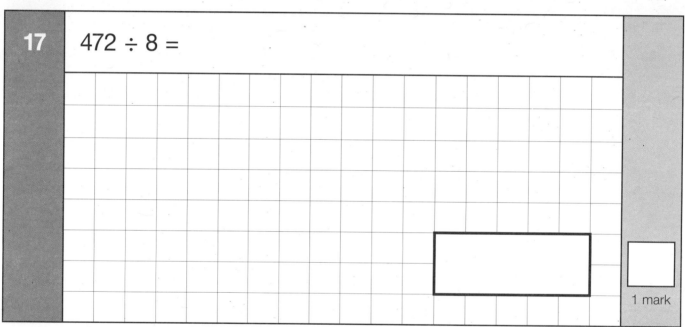

1 mark

18 0.08 ÷ 10 =

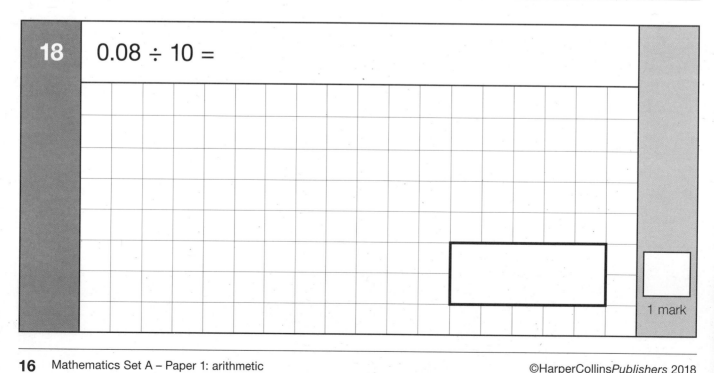

1 mark

19 $3{,}465 \times 1{,}000 =$

20

| 1 | 9 | 6 | 0 | 8 |

Show your method

21 $8 - 2.64 =$

22

```
    5 3 7 5
×       3 6
```

Show your method

2 marks

23

$$\frac{2}{5} - \frac{3}{10} =$$

1 mark

24

```
    5 2 7
×     6 2
```

Show your method

2 marks

25 45.9 − 23.739 =

1 mark

26 $\dfrac{1}{3} + \dfrac{1}{6} + \dfrac{1}{10} =$

1 mark

27 $\dfrac{3}{8} \div 3 =$

1 mark

28 $\dfrac{5}{6} \div 2 =$

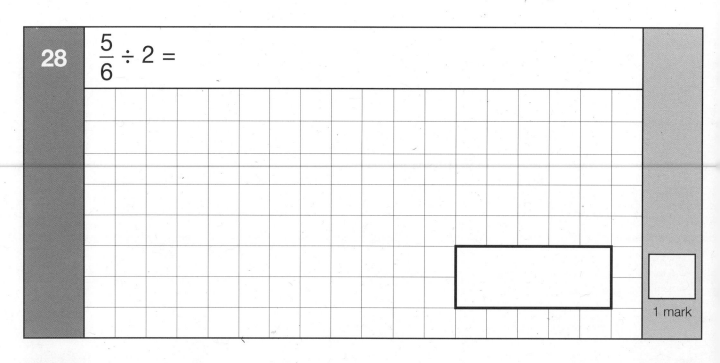

1 mark

29 35% of 520 =

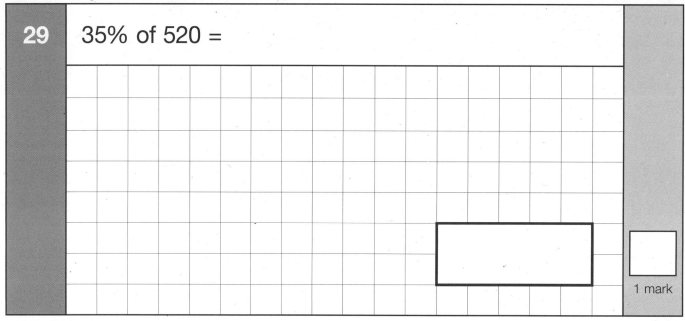

1 mark

30 $3\dfrac{2}{5} + \dfrac{7}{10} =$

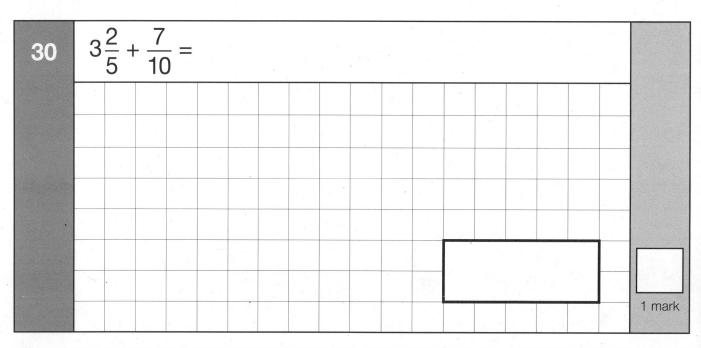

1 mark

31 8% of 700 =

1 mark

32 $3\dfrac{5}{8} + 1\dfrac{2}{3} =$

1 mark

33 0.6 × 300 =

1 mark

34 12% × 2,000 =

1 mark

35 $1\frac{1}{2} \times 63 =$

1 mark

36

4 7 | 1 8 3 3

Show your method

2 marks

This is a blank page

This is a blank page

Key Stage 2

Mathematics
Set A

Paper 2: reasoning

Name							
School							
Date of Birth	Day		Month		Year		

Instructions

Do not use a calculator to answer the questions in this test.

Questions and answers

You have **40 minutes** to complete this test.

Follow the instructions carefully for each question.

If you need to do working out, use the space around the question.

Some questions have a method box. For these questions, you may get one mark for showing the correct method.

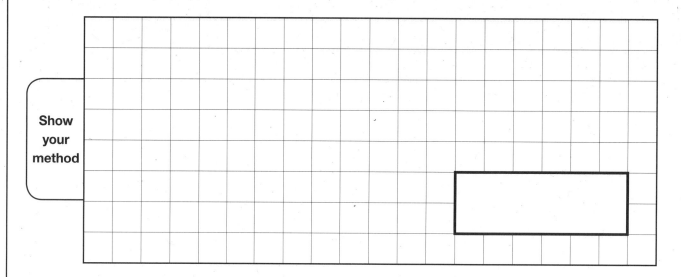

Show your method

If you cannot do a question, move on to the next one, then go back to it at the end if you have time.

If you finish before the end of the test, go back and check your answers.

Marks

The numbers under the boxes at the side of the page tell you the number of marks for each question.

1 Sara asked the children in Year 3 and Year 5 if they had a pet.

This graph shows the results.

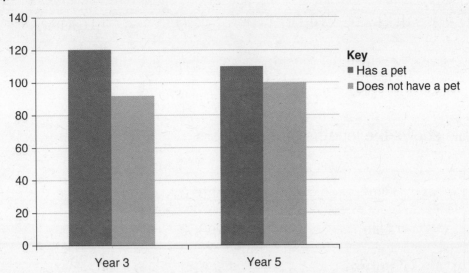

Altogether, how many children do not have a pet?

1 mark

How many more Year 3 children than Year 5 children have a pet?

1 mark

2 Write the missing numbers to make this multiplication grid correct.

X		
8	72	40
	108	60

1 mark

3 Circle the number that is ten times greater than four hundred and three.

4,300   403   4,003   430   4,030

1 mark

4 This table shows the lengths of three rivers.

River	Length in km
Nile	6,853
Zambezi	2,693
Loire	1,012

How much longer is the river Nile than the combined length of the other two rivers?

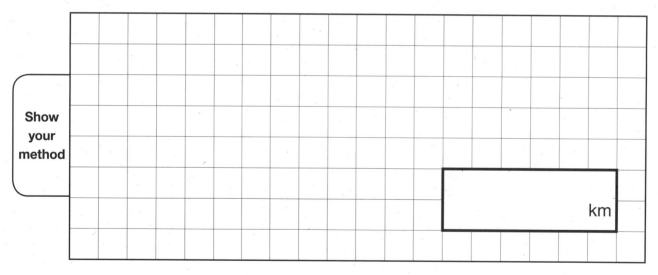

Show your method

km

2 marks

5 Amy arrives at a railway station at 11:40 am to catch a train.

She waits 22 minutes for her train to leave.

The journey takes $2\frac{1}{4}$ hours.

When will she arrive at her destination?

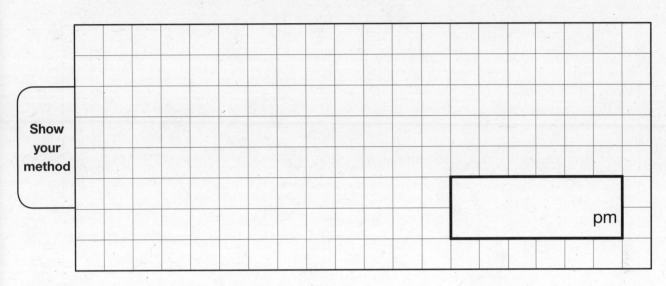

Show your method

pm

2 marks

6 A concert is going to be held in a stadium.

The tickets are put up for sale.

26 tickets are sold in the first hour.

By the end of the day 1,000 more tickets have been sold.

How many tickets have been sold in total?

tickets

1 mark

After one week, 17,269 tickets have been sold.

1,000 tickets were sold at half price.

How many tickets have been sold at full price?

tickets

1 mark

7 At the start of May, there were 1,576 tennis balls in the sports shop.

During May,

- 9,854 more tennis balls were delivered

- 8,546 tennis balls were sold.

How many tennis balls were left in the shop at the end of May?

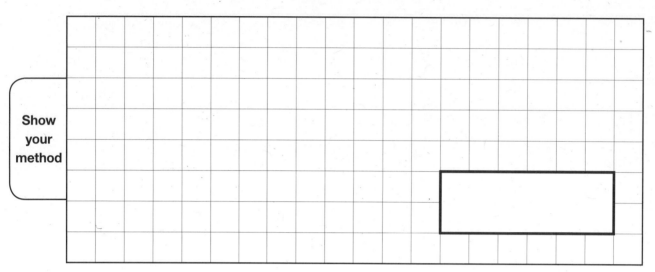

Show your method

2 marks

8 Tick **two** shapes that have $\frac{3}{4}$ shaded.

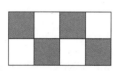

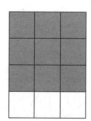

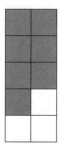

1 mark

9 Here is a rule for the time it takes to cook roast beef.

Cooking time = 30 minutes plus an extra 20 minutes for each kilogram

How many minutes will it take to cook a 4 kg joint of beef?

minutes

1 mark

What is the mass of a joint of beef that takes 90 minutes to cook?

kg

1 mark

10 Tick the **two** numbers that are equivalent to $\frac{1}{5}$

0.15 ☐

0.2 ☐

$\frac{15}{100}$ ☐

$\frac{4}{20}$ ☐

1.5 ☐

2 marks

11 Here are diagrams of some 3-D shapes.

Tick each shape which has more vertices than faces.

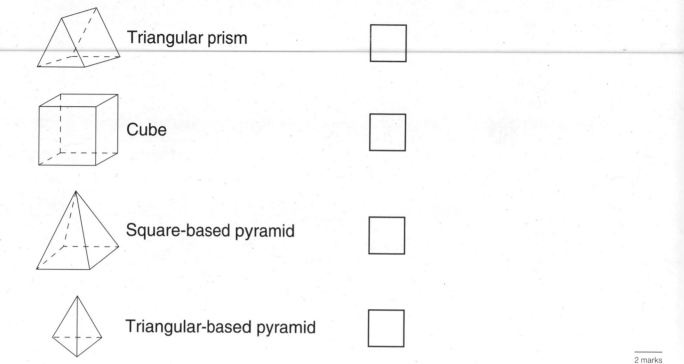

Triangular prism ☐

Cube ☐

Square-based pyramid ☐

Triangular-based pyramid ☐

2 marks

12 Write these numbers in order of size, starting with the **smallest**.

2.5   0.72   2.134   0.428

1 mark

13 Kate and Daniel buy some lollies.

Box of 12 lollies

12 lollies

£10.49

95p each

Kate buys a pack of 12 lollies for £10.49

Daniel buys 12 single lollies for 95p each.

How much more does Daniel pay than Kate?

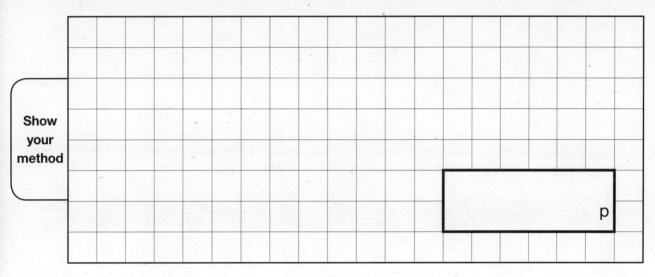

Show your method

p

2 marks

14 At the end of a TV programme, the year it was made is given in Roman numerals.

MMXII

Write the year MMXII in figures.

1 mark

15 Amy poured some drinks at a party.

For every 4 drinks Amy poured, only 3 were drunk.

Altogether, 15 drinks were drunk.

How many drinks did Amy pour?

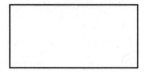

16 Craig spins this spinner:

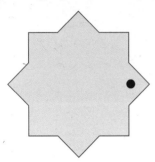

The spinner completes one-and-a-half turns before it stops.

Draw the new position of the dot on this spinner:

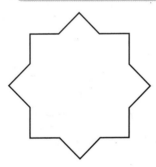

17 Amina posts three parcels.

The postage costs the same for each parcel.

She pays with a £20 note.

Her change is £14.81

What is the cost of posting one parcel?

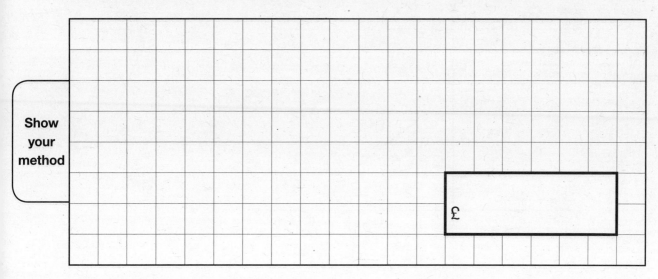

Show your method

£

2 marks

18 Ben has driven 20 kilometres.

10% of his journey has been completed.

Write the missing percentage.

Ben has driven 30 kilometres.

% of his journey has been completed.

1 mark

19 The vertices of a quadrilateral have these coordinates.

(2, 5) (6, 2) (1, –7) (–6, 5)

One side of the quadrilateral has been drawn on the grid.

Complete the quadrilateral.

Use a ruler.

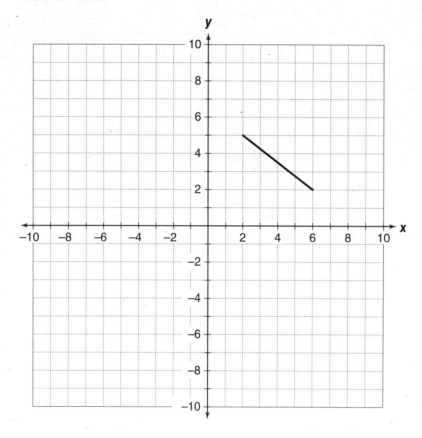

1 mark

20 Samir says

'4,052,234 is smaller than 967,358 because the digits are smaller.'

Explain why he is incorrect.

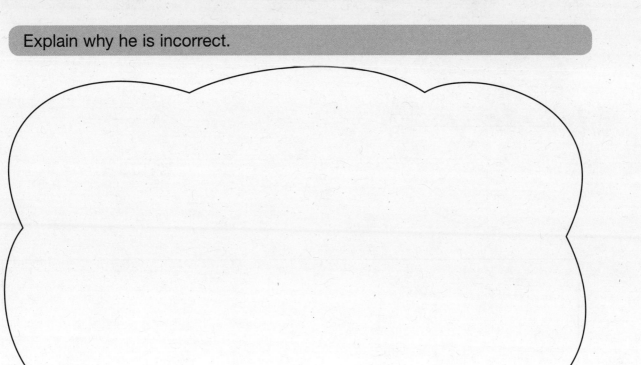

1 mark

21 On a map, 1 cm represents 50 km.

The distance between two towns is 775 km.

On the map, what is the measurement in cm between the two towns?

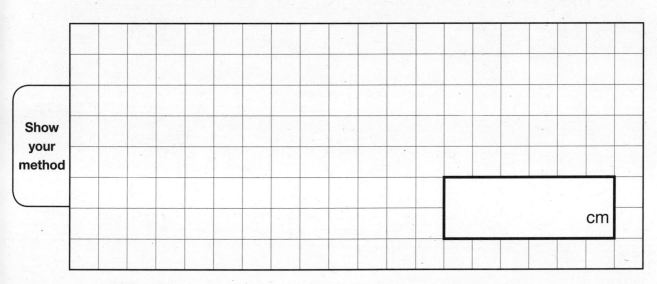

Show your method

cm

2 marks

22. In this circle, $\frac{1}{4}$ and $\frac{1}{8}$ are shaded.

What fraction of the whole circle is **not** shaded?

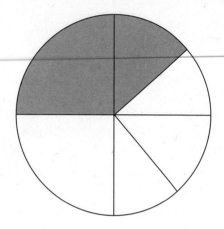

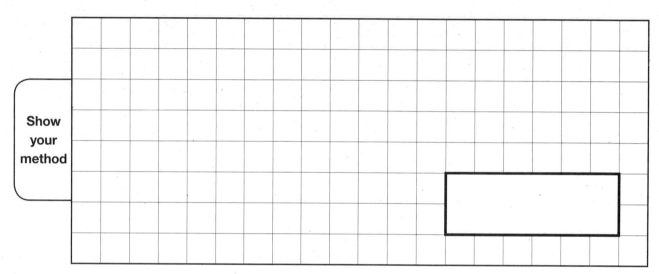

Show your method

2 marks

23 Here are two similar quadrilaterals.

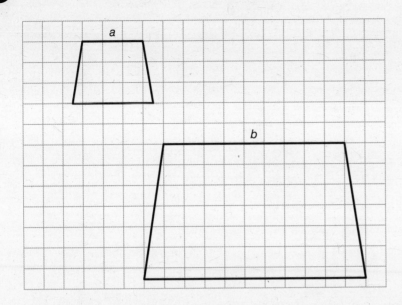

Write the ratio of side *a* to side *b*.

1 mark

This is a blank page

Key Stage 2

Mathematics
Set A
Paper 3: reasoning

Name						
School						
Date of Birth	Day		Month		Year	

Instructions

Do not use a calculator to answer the questions in this test.

Questions and answers

You have **40 minutes** to complete this test.

Follow the instructions carefully for each question.

If you need to do working out, use the space around the question.

Some questions have a method box. For these questions, you may get one mark for showing the correct method.

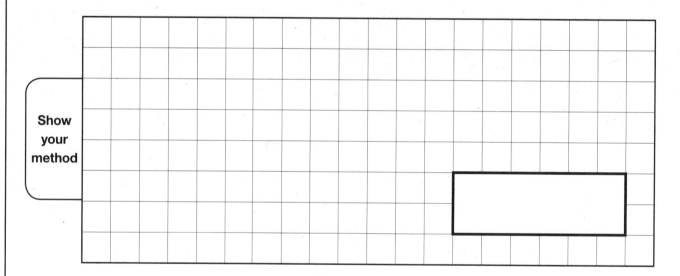

Show your method

If you cannot do a question, move on to the next one, then go back to it at the end if you have time.

If you finish before the end of the test, go back and check your answers.

Marks

The numbers under the boxes at the side of the page tell you the number of marks for each question.

1 Put these sports car prices in order, starting with the **lowest price**.

One has been done for you.

A — £147,250

B — £104,150

C — £140,500

D — £151,600

E — £87,500

	B			

2 Ali puts these five numbers in their correct places on a number line.

709   698   703   771   638

Write the number closest to 700

Write the number furthest from 700

3 Write the three missing digits to make this addition correct.

$$
\begin{array}{cccc}
 & 2 & 7 & \boxed{} \\
+ & 5 & \boxed{} & 2 \\
\hline
\boxed{} & & 2 & 6 \\
\end{array}
$$

2 marks

4 Write each number in its correct place on the diagram.

19   21   23   25

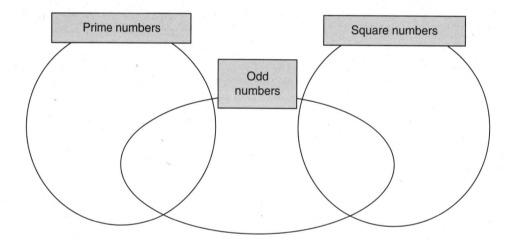

2 marks

5 A teacher buys 4 large boxes of pens and 3 small boxes of pens.

Each large box has 60 pens.

Each small box has 30 pens.

How many pens did the teacher buy altogether?

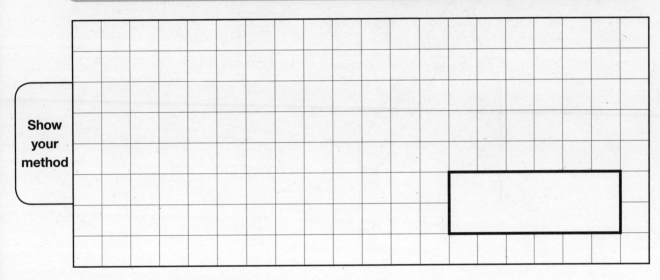

Show
your
method

2 marks

6 This diagram shows a shaded shape inside a border of squares.

> Draw the reflection of the shape in the mirror line.

Use a ruler.

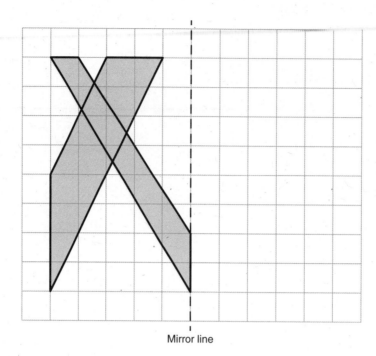

Mirror line

1 mark

7 Write the two missing values to make these equivalent fractions correct.

$$\frac{\Box}{5} = \frac{8}{10} = \frac{16}{\Box}$$

2 marks

8 Circle **two** numbers that add together to equal 0.37

0.07　　　0.33　　　0.3　　　0.7

1 mark

9 10 pens cost £1.90

5 pens and 1 ruler cost £1.32

What is the cost of 1 ruler?

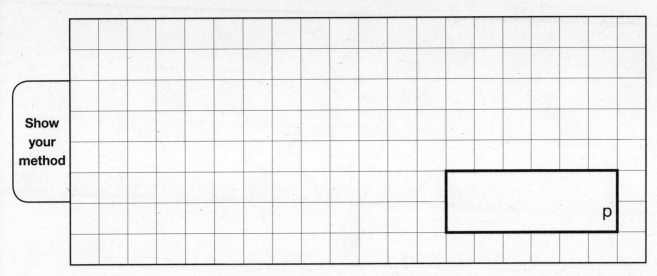

Show
your
method

p

2 marks

10 Each diagram below is divided into equal sections.

Shade two-fifths of each diagram.

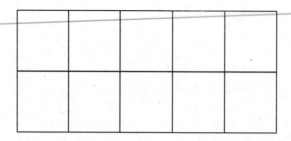

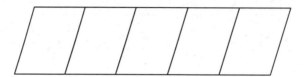

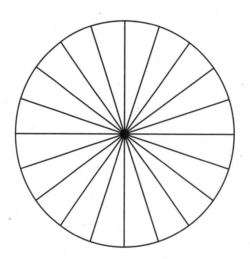

2 marks

11 A packet contains 1.5 kg of cereal.

Every day Maria eats 30 g of cereal.

How many days does the packet of cereal last?

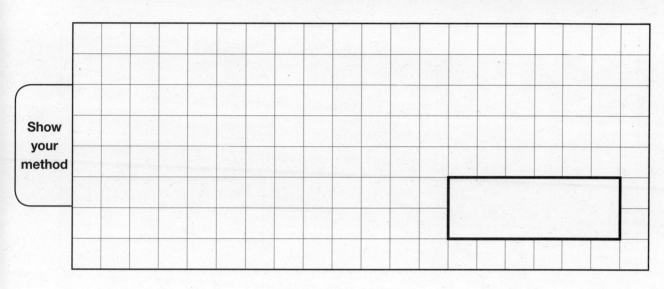

Show your method

2 marks

12 $x = 34$

What is $2x + 8$?

1 mark

$3z + 20 = 110$

Work out the value of z.

1 mark

13 After a sports day, $27\frac{3}{4}$ bags of rubbish are collected.

The mean mass of a bag is 13 kg.

What is the total mass, in kg, of rubbish collected?

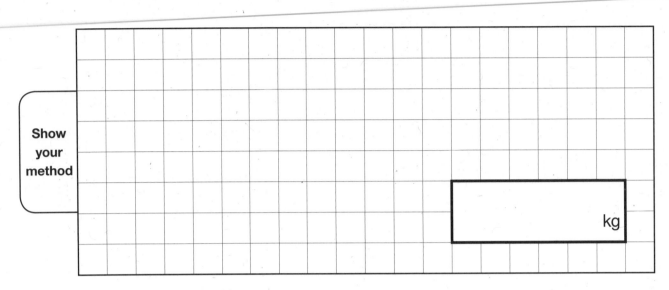

Show your method

kg

2 marks

14 Write all the common multiples of 6 and 9 that are less than 50

1 mark

15 This thermometer shows temperatures in both °C and °F.

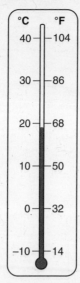

Work out what 35 °C is in °F.

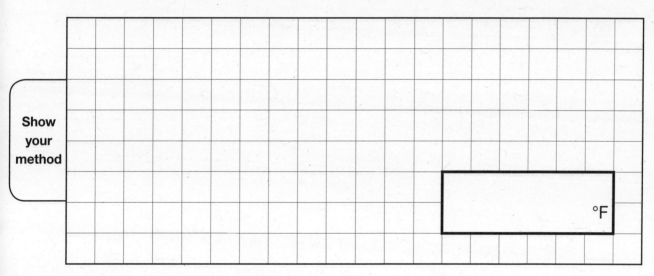

Show your method

°F

2 marks

16 Calculate the size of angles *a* and *b* in this diagram.

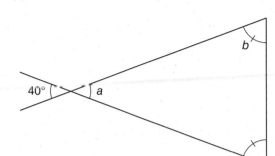

$a =$ [   ] $b =$ [   ]

2 marks

17 Write the number that is ten less than nine million.

[   ]

1 mark

18 A factory loads 500 cans of drink into crates.

2.5 crates are filled.

How many cans of drink are in one full crate?

cans

1 mark

19 Miss Smith is making jam to sell at the school fair.

Raspberries cost £8.50 per kg.

Sugar costs 85p per kg.

10 glass jars cost £7.50

She uses 12 kg of raspberries and 12 kg of sugar to make 20 jars full of jam.

Calculate the total cost to make 20 jars full of jam.

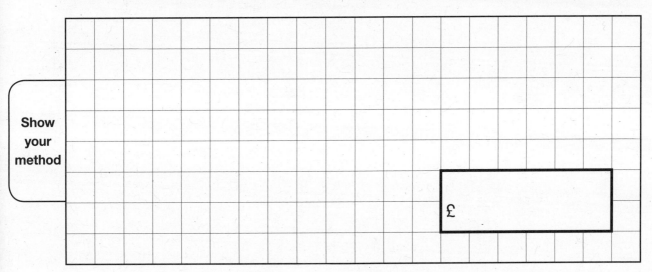

Show
your
method

£

3 marks

20 Here are two triangles drawn on coordinate axes.

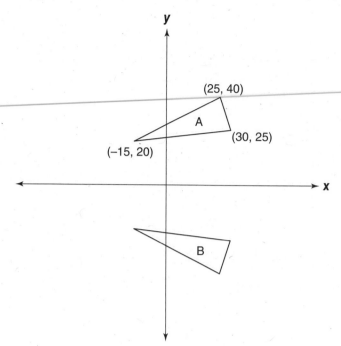

Triangle B is a reflection of triangle A in the x-axis.

Two of the new vertices of triangle B are (30, −25) and (25, −40).

What are the coordinates of the third vertex of triangle B?

1 mark

21 Each shape stands for a positive whole number.

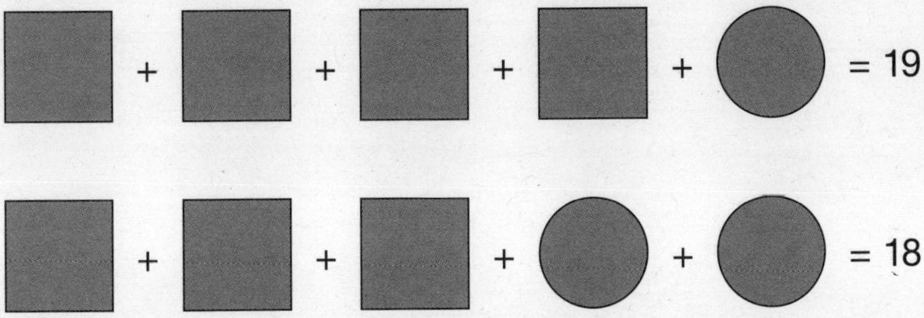

$$\square + \square + \square + \square + \bigcirc = 19$$

$$\square + \square + \square + \bigcirc + \bigcirc = 18$$

Find the value of each shape.

$\square$ =

$\bigcirc$ =

1 mark

This is a blank page

Key Stage 2

Mathematics
Set B

Paper 1: arithmetic

Name	
School	
Date of Birth	Day		Month		Year	

Instructions

Do not use a calculator to answer the questions in this test.

Questions and answers

You have **30 minutes** to complete this test.

Write your answer in the box provided for each question.

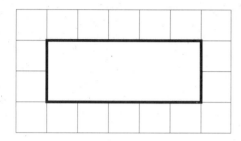

You should give all answers as a single value.

For questions expressed as mixed numbers or common fractions, you should give your answers as mixed numbers or common fractions.

If you cannot do a question, move on to the next one, then go back to it at the end if you have time.

If you finish before the end of the test, go back and check your answers.

Marks

The numbers under the boxes at the side of the page tell you the number of marks for each question.

Answers are worth one or two marks.

Long division and long multiplication questions are worth **TWO marks each**. You will get TWO marks for a correct answer; you may get **ONE mark** for showing a correct method.

1 953 + 100 =

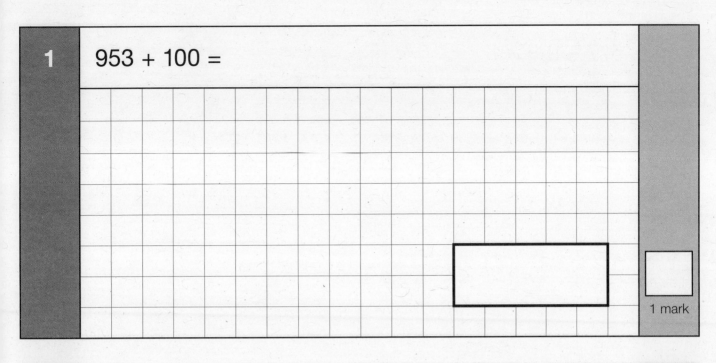

1 mark

2 35 + 407 =

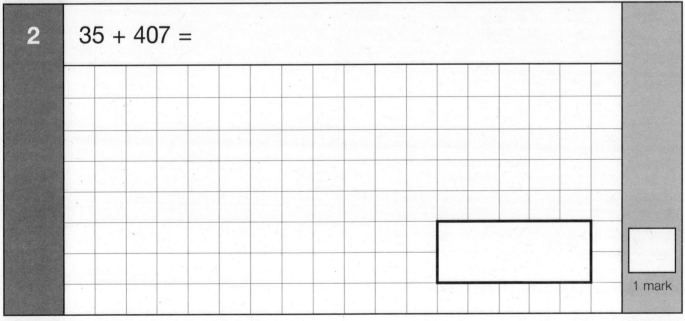

1 mark

3 2,300 × 5 =

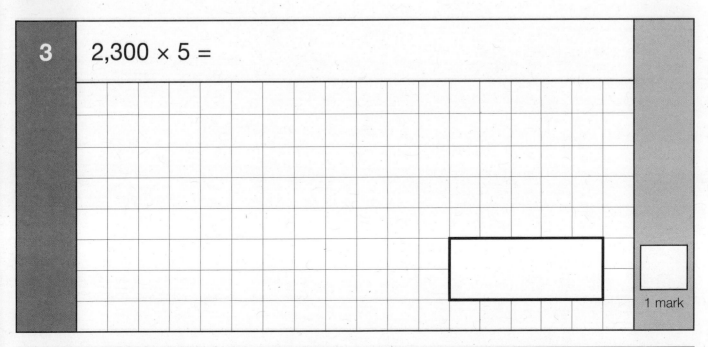

1 mark

4 577 − 9 =

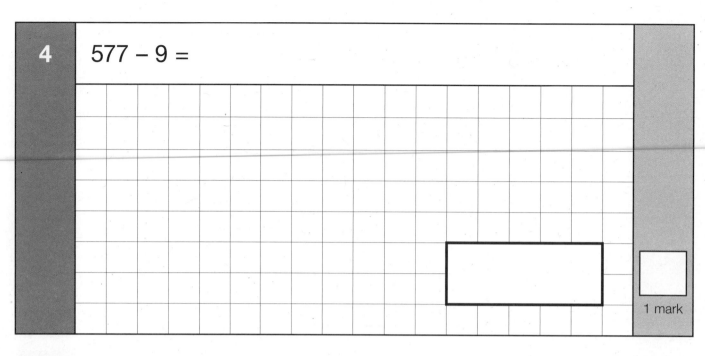

1 mark

5 _____ = 864 + 355

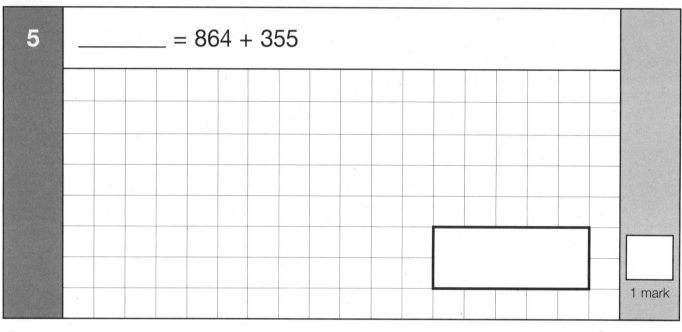

1 mark

6 98 ÷ 7 =

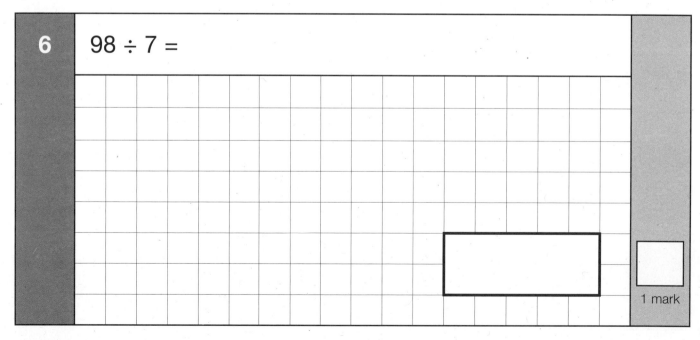

1 mark

7 $4 \times 7 \times 10 =$

1 mark

8   _____ $= 659 - 50$

1 mark

9 $124 \div 4 =$

1 mark

10 756 × 3 =

1 mark

11 62 × 9 =

1 mark

12 40 × 80 =

1 mark

13 $\frac{2}{5}$ of 2,000

1 mark

14 6.009 + 2.34 =

1 mark

15 525 ÷ 3 =

1 mark

16   12.97 + 31.428 =

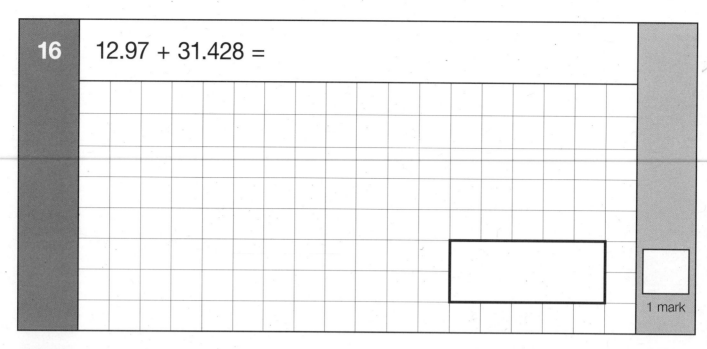

1 mark

17   258.37 − 69.4 =

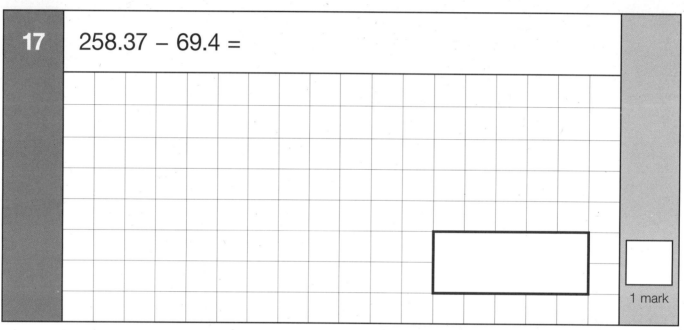

1 mark

18   243,327 − 12,998 =

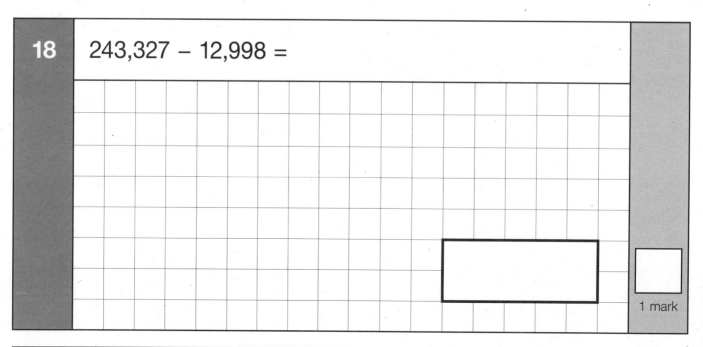

1 mark

19 $4^2 + 20 =$

1 mark

20 $0.3 \div 10 =$

1 mark

21 $6 - 2.25 =$

1 mark

22 $1,210 \div 11 =$

1 mark

23

Show your method

$$\begin{array}{r} 3\ 8\ 1 \\ \times\quad 3\ 7 \\ \hline \end{array}$$

2 marks

24 $\dfrac{4}{9} + \dfrac{7}{9} =$

1 mark

25 30% of 2,700 =

26 15 × 4.3 =

27 $\dfrac{2}{5} - \dfrac{1}{15} =$

28

$3\,4\,\overline{)8\,8\,4}$

Show
your
method

2 marks

29

15% of 620 =

1 mark

30

$$\begin{array}{r} 7\ 4\ 6\ 9 \\ \times\ \ \ \ \ 4\ 2 \\ \hline \end{array}$$

Show
your
method

2 marks

31

$$1\frac{7}{10} - \frac{3}{20} =$$

1 mark

32

2 3 | 1 1 7 3

Show your method

2 marks

33

$$\frac{4}{7} \div 4 =$$

1 mark

34 $\dfrac{3}{10} \times 120 =$

1 mark

35 $4\dfrac{1}{3} - 2\dfrac{3}{4} =$

1 mark

36 $80 + 64 \div 8 =$

1 mark

This is a blank page

This is a blank page

Key Stage 2

Mathematics
Set B

Paper 2: reasoning

Name						
School						
Date of Birth	Day		Month		Year	

Instructions

Do not use a calculator to answer the questions in this test.

Questions and answers

You have **40 minutes** to complete this test.

Follow the instructions carefully for each question.

If you need to do working out, use the space around the question.

Some questions have a method box. For these questions, you may get one mark for showing the correct method.

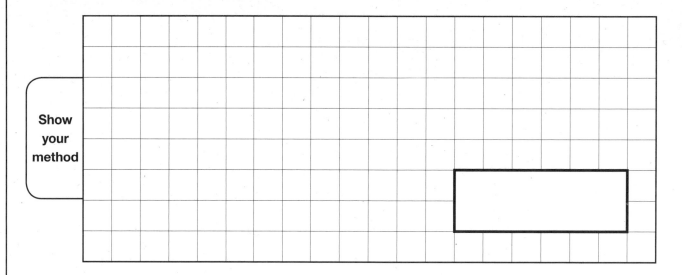

Show your method

If you cannot do a question, move on to the next one, then go back to it at the end if you have time.

If you finish before the end of the test, go back and check your answers.

Marks

The numbers under the boxes at the side of the page tell you the number of marks for each question.

1 A clock shows this time twice a day.

Tick the two digital clocks that show this time.

07:50   08:50   19:50   10:50   20:50

1 mark

2 Sam completes this calculation.

```
  6 4
+ 2 8
─────
  9 2
```

Write a **subtraction** calculation he could use to check his answer.

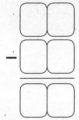

1 mark

Sam then completes this calculation.

```
  8 5
- 3 8
─────
  4 7
```

Write a **subtraction** calculation he could use to check his answer.

1 mark

3 The numbers in this sequence increase by 16 each time.

| | 77 | 93 | | 125 | 141 | |

2 marks

4 Each shape stands for a number.

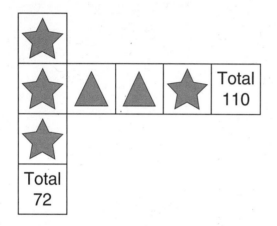

Work out the value of each shape.

△ =

⭐ =

2 marks

5 Write these numbers in order, starting with the **smallest**.

0.89　　0.509　　4.8　　0.079　　3.001

1 mark

6 Jackie cuts 6 metres of rope into three pieces.

The length of the first piece is 2.45 metres.

The length of the second piece is 1.85 metres.

Work out the length of the third piece.

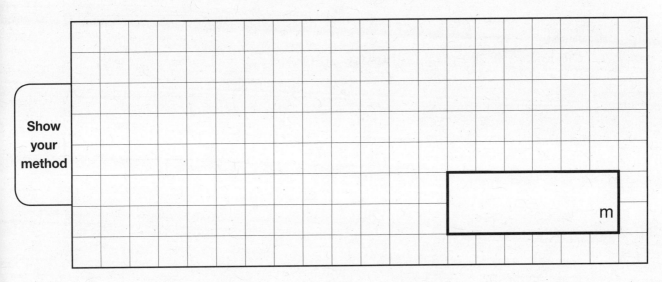

Show your method

m

2 marks

7 Here are five angles.

Write the letters of the angles that are obtuse.

Write the letters of the angles that are acute.

8 Asha buys three packets of crisps.

She pays with a £2 coin.

This is her change.

What is the cost of one packet of crisps?

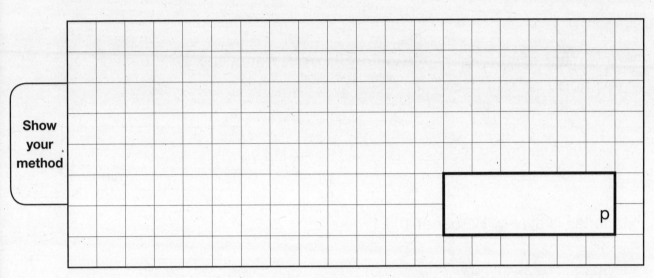

Show your method

p

2 marks

9 Here is part of the bus timetable from Greenvale to Riverford.

Greenvale	09:51	10:02	10:17	10:34
Winchley	09:59	10:10	10:24	10:41
New Harper	10:19	10:30	10:45	11:02
Mountsford	10:24	10:35	10:52	11:09
Riverford	10:34	10:45	11:04	11:21

How many minutes does it take the 10:17 bus from Greenvale to reach Riverford?

minutes

1 mark

Mr Jones is at New Harper at 10:21

What is the earliest time he can reach Riverford on the bus?

1 mark

10 A sweet shop orders 12 boxes of chocolates.

Each box contains 8 bags of chocolates.

Each bag contains 50 chocolates.

How many chocolates does the shop order in total?

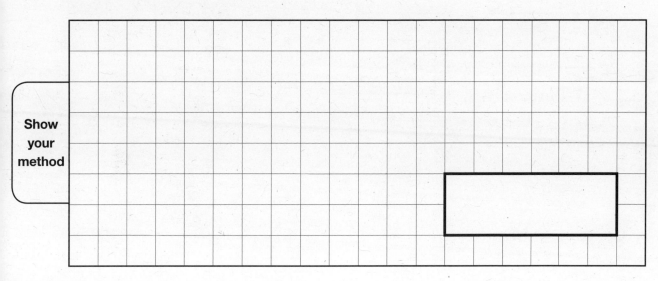

Show your method

2 marks

11 Fay uses one centimetre cubes to make these cuboids.

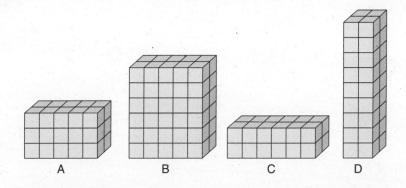

A   B   C   D

Which cuboid uses the greatest number of centimetre cubes?

1 mark

12 A triangle is translated from position A to position B.

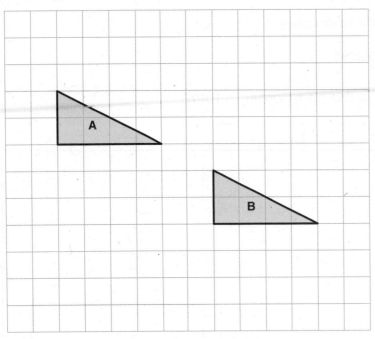

Complete the sentence.

The triangle has moved [ ] squares to the right and [ ]

squares down.

1 mark

13 Complete each sentence using a number from the list below.

1,200   2,400   600   7,200   3,600   480

There are [ ] minutes in eight hours.

1 mark

There are [ ] seconds in two hours.

1 mark

14 Lara chooses a number less than 30

She divides it by 4 and then adds 8

She then divides this result by 4

Her answer is 3.5

What was the number she started with?

Show your method

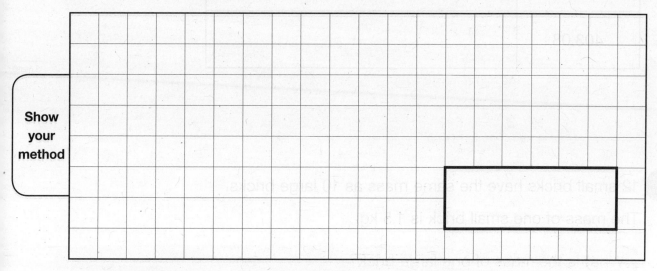

2 marks

15 A factory produces **2 million** cans of drink a day.

Tick the correct statement about the factory.

The factory fills 5,000 boxes with 40 cans a day. ☐

The factory fills 50,000 boxes with 4 cans a day. ☐

The factory fills 50,000 boxes with 40 cans a day. ☐

The factory fills 50,000 boxes with 400 cans a day. ☐

The factory fills 50,000 boxes with 4,000 cans a day. ☐

1 mark

16 Complete this table by rounding the numbers to the nearest hundred.

	Rounded to the nearest hundred
40,901	
4,080.5	
403.08	

2 marks

17 12 small bricks have the same mass as 10 large bricks.

The mass of one small brick is 1.5 kg.

What is the mass of one large brick?

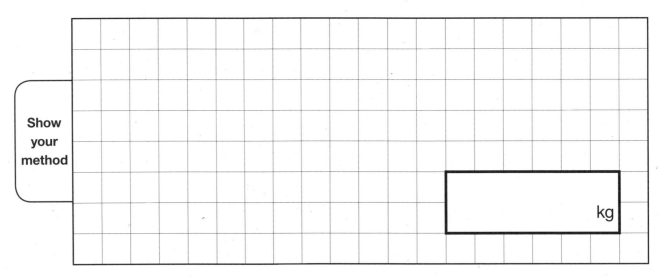

Show your method

kg

2 marks

18 Sam finished a cycle race in 32 minutes 42 seconds.

Ollie finished 2 minutes 20 seconds after Sam.

How long did Ollie take?

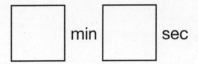

min ☐ sec

1 mark

Mia finished the race 3 minutes 18 seconds before Sam.

How long did Mia take?

☐ min ☐ sec

1 mark

19 Here are five quadrilaterals on a square grid.

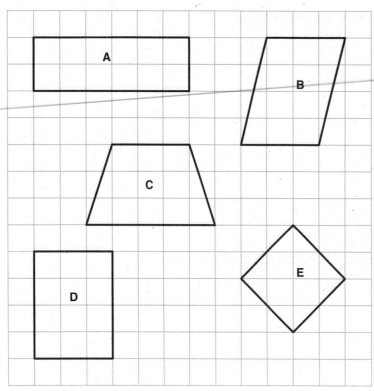

Four of the quadrilaterals have the same area.

Which quadrilateral has a different area?

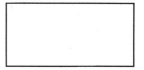

1 mark

20 Lara had some money.

She spent £1.75 on a bus ticket.

She spent £2.55 on her lunch.

She has two-thirds of her money left.

How much money did Lara have to start with?

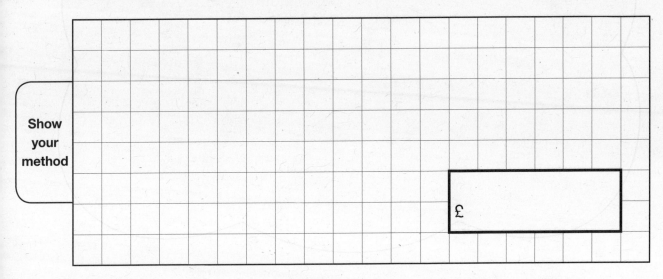

Show your method

£

21 $6{,}832 \div 16 = 427$

Explain how you can use this fact to find the answer to 17×427

1 mark

Key Stage 2

Mathematics
Set B

Paper 3: reasoning

Name						
School						
Date of Birth	Day		Month		Year	

Instructions

Do not use a calculator to answer the questions in this test.

Questions and answers

You have **40 minutes** to complete this test.

Follow the instructions carefully for each question.

If you need to do working out, use the space around the question.

Some questions have a method box. For these questions, you may get one mark for showing the correct method.

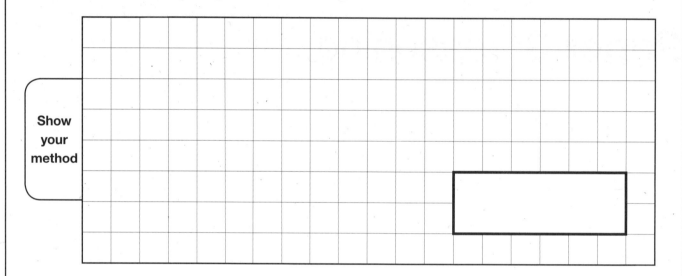

Show your method

If you cannot do a question, move on to the next one, then go back to it at the end if you have time.

If you finish before the end of the test, go back and check your answers.

Marks

The numbers under the boxes at the side of the page tell you the number of marks for each question.

1 Write the missing number to make this division correct.

$15 \div \boxed{} = 0.15$

1 mark

2 Cody uses these digit cards.

5   4   7

He makes a 2-digit number and a 1-digit number.

He multiplies them together.

His answer is a multiple of 10

What could Cody's multiplication be?

    ×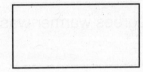

1 mark

3 A group of friends earns £114 by doing odd jobs.

They share the money equally.

Each friend gets £19

How many friends are in the group?

1 mark

4 This graph shows the temperature in °C from 2 am to 3 pm on a cold day.

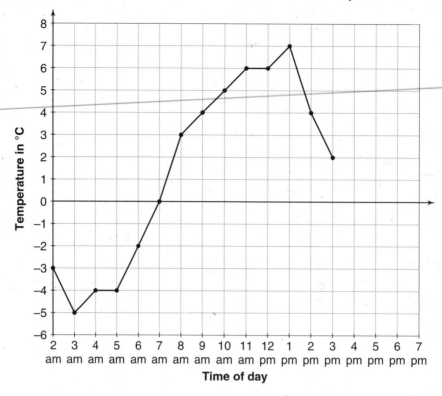

Time of day

How many degrees warmer was it at 12 pm than at 4 am?

°C

1 mark

At 7 pm the temperature was 8 degrees lower than at 2 pm.

What was the temperature at 7 pm?

°C

1 mark

5 Sue wants to travel to London by plane.

She needs to arrive in London by 4:30 pm.

Circle the latest flight that Sue can take.

Flight from Edinburgh	Arrives in London
12:15	13:30
13:15	14:30
14:25	15:47
15:25	16:40
17:15	18:25
18:40	19:55
20:05	21:40

1 mark

6 Charlie is saving up for a new phone.

He needs to save £250

So far he has saved £28.81

How much more does he need to save?

1 mark

7 Here is a triangle drawn on a coordinate grid.

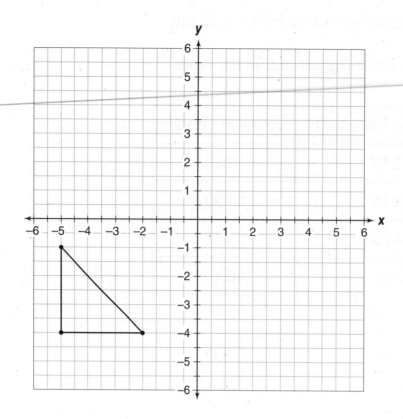

The triangle is translated 6 right and 7 up.

Draw the triangle in its new position.

1 mark

8 Write three factors of 40 that are not factors of 16

9 Here is the timetable for fitness sessions at the leisure centre.

	Monday	Tuesday	Wednesday	Thursday	Friday
9:00 – 10:30	Aquacise	Zumba	Spinning	Aquacise	Spinning
10:30 – 11:30	Spinning	Aquacise	Zumba	Zumba	Aquacise
11:30 – 12:00	Zumba	Aquacise	Spinning	Aquacise	Zumba

What is the **total** number of hours for **Aquacise** classes on this timetable?

1 mark

©HarperCollins*Publishers* 2018   Mathematics Set B – Paper 3: reasoning   **95**

10 A car steering wheel has a diameter of 32 cm.

What is the radius of the steering wheel?

cm

11 A bottle contains 768 millilitres of juice.

Jane pours out a quarter of a litre.

How much juice is left?

ml

12 Circle the hexagon which has exactly two acute angles.

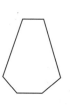

13 Clara buys 4 packs of chocolate biscuits.

Harry buys 2 packs of vanilla biscuits.

Packet of 32 chocolate biscuits   Packet of 16 vanilla biscuits

Clara says,

'I have four times as many biscuits as Harry.'

| Explain why Clara is correct. |

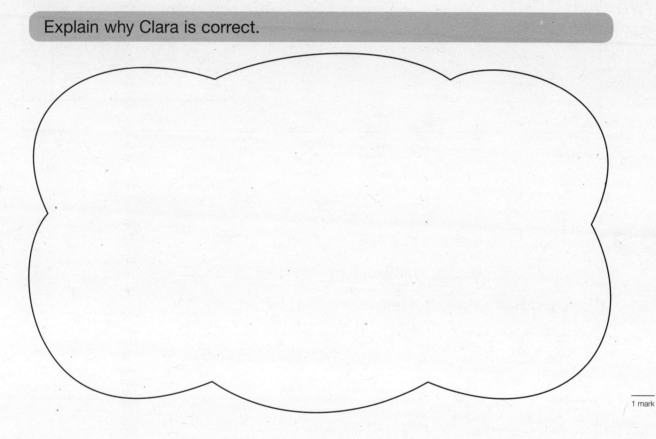

1 mark

14 5 pineapples cost the same as 4 coconuts.

One coconut costs £1.65

How much does one pineapple cost?

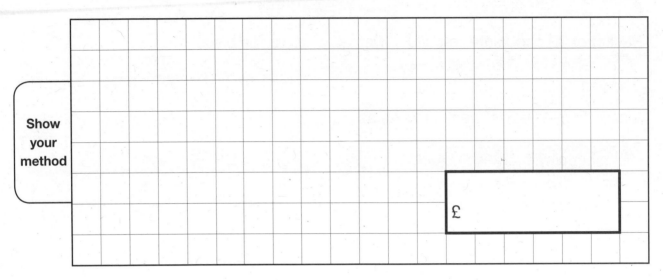

£

2 marks

15 There are 3,200 marbles in a box.

Ivan and Sam take 350 marbles each.

Clara and Harry share the rest of the marbles equally.

How many marbles does Clara get?

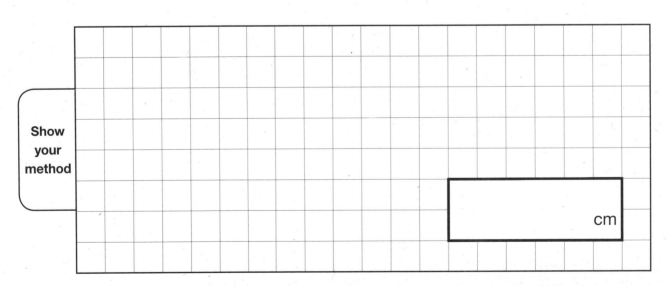

cm

2 marks

16 Look at the letters below.

Circle the letter below that has both parallel and perpendicular lines.

H   J   T   X   C

1 mark

17 Amy has £800

She spends 45% of her money on a new laptop.

How much does Amy spend on her new computer?

£

1 mark

18 An aeroplane is 75 metres long and has a wingspan of 60 metres.

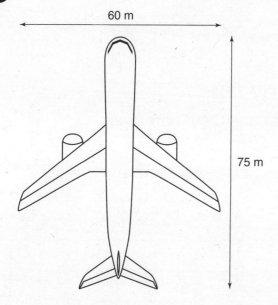

60 m

75 m

Not to scale

Josh makes a model of the aeroplane.

His model is 25 cm long.

What is the wingspan of the model?

cm

1 mark

19 Polly wants to estimate the answer to this calculation.

$$5\frac{3}{8} + 2\frac{5}{6} + 3\frac{5}{12} =$$

Tick the calculation that is the best estimate.

5 + 2 + 3 ☐

5 + 3 + 3 ☐

5 + 2 + 2 ☐

6 + 2 + 3 ☐

6 + 3 + 3 ☐

1 mark

20 A square of paper measures 30 cm by 30 cm.

A rectangular piece of paper is 4 cm **longer** and 3 cm **narrower** than the square piece.

What is the **difference in area** between the two pieces?

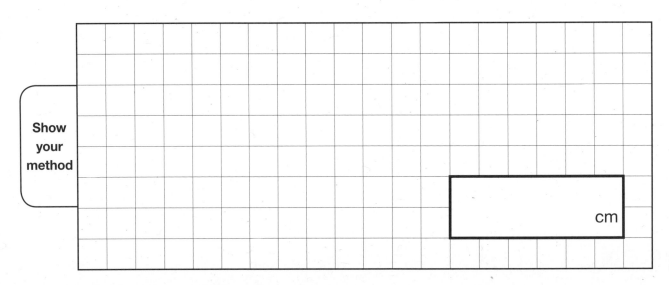

Show your method

cm

3 marks

21 Harry thinks of a whole number.

He multiplies it by 6

He rounds his answer to the nearest 10

The result is 70

Write all the possible numbers that Harry could have started with.

2 marks

22 The numbers in this sequence increase by the same amount each time.

Write the missing numbers.

1    $1\frac{6}{8}$ $2\frac{1}{2}$

2 marks

23 In this diagram, the shaded rectangles are all of equal width (w).

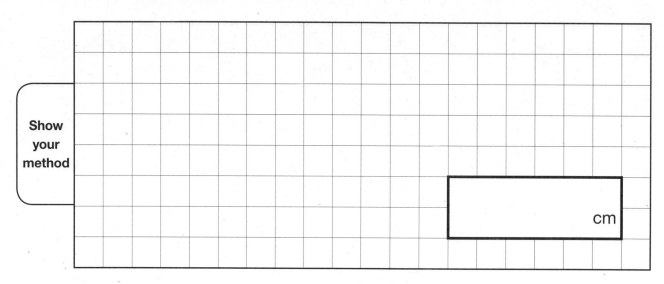

Calculate the width (w) of one shaded rectangle.

Show your method

cm

2 marks

24 Cube A and cuboid B have the same volume.

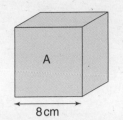

8 cm

2 cm

B

?

8 cm

Calculate the missing length on cuboid B.

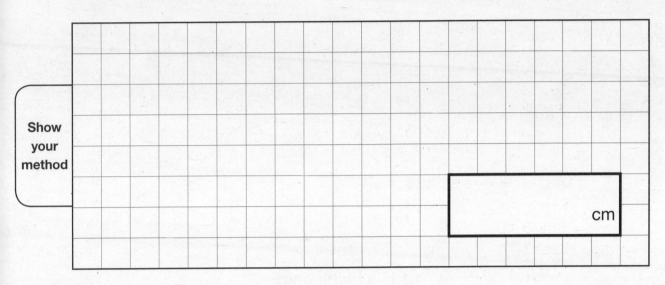

Show your method

cm

2 marks

25 Here is a pattern of number pairs.

a	b
2	6
3	10
4	14
5	18

Complete the rule for the number pattern.

b = ☐ × a − ☐

1 mark

This is a blank page

Key Stage 2 English Practice Papers
Contents, Instructions and Answers

Author: Faisal Nasim

Contents

Instructions

Introduction

This practice resource consists of two complete sets of Key Stage 2 English practice test papers. Each set contains similar test papers to those that pupils will take at the end of Year 6:

- **Reading** – each test is made up of three different texts (in a reading booklet), and an answer booklet.
- **Grammar, Punctuation and Spelling** – each test is made up of Paper 1 and Paper 2. Paper 1 contains 50 questions; Paper 2 contains 20 spellings. The spelling test administration guide can be found on pages 9 and 16 of this answers booklet.

These test papers can be used any time throughout the year to provide practice for the Key Stage 2 tests.

Administering the Tests

- Children should work in a quiet environment where they can complete each test undisturbed.
- The amount of time per test varies, so children should check the time given on each test paper.
- Handwriting is not assessed but children should write their answers clearly.

Marking the Tests

Each set of English practice papers contains a Reading paper and two Grammar, punctuation and spelling papers:

- Reading is worth 50 marks
- Grammar, punctuation and spelling Paper 1 is worth 50 marks ⎫
- Grammar, punctuation and spelling Paper 2 is worth 20 marks ⎬ Total = 70 marks

Use this answer booklet to mark the test papers.

Add up the total marks for the Reading paper. As a general guideline, if a child gets 26 or more marks on the Reading paper (i.e. 28 or more out of 50), they are reaching the expected standard.

Add up the total marks for the Grammar, punctuation and spelling Paper 1 and Grammar, punctuation and spelling Paper 2. As a general guideline, if a child gets 38 or more marks across the two papers (i.e. 38 or more out of 70), they are reaching the expected standard.

Keep in mind that the exact number of marks required to achieve the expected standard may vary year by year depending on the overall difficulty of the test.

Answers

Set A Reading

Content domain coverage for the questions in this paper are shown in the table of answers below. Information about these codes can be found in the KS2 English Reading test framework.

Question (Content domain)		Requirement	Mark
1	(2d)	Award 1 mark for **It is raining.**	1
2	(2a)	Award 1 mark for **indulged**	1
3	(2b)	Award 1 mark for reference to any of the following: • Peter hasn't got any Pickeez. • Peter isn't getting the new toys at the same time as his friends. • Peter's mother sometimes tells him 'no'. • Peter has asked for a new toy but hasn't received it. Do not accept any reference to the weather, Peter's boring day or his having to walk through puddles.	1
4	(2d)	Award 1 mark for a reference to Peter being in a bad mood or specifically a bad mood with his mother or that he wanted her to feel guilty, e.g. • Peter was cross because he couldn't have the Pickeez. • Peter was mad at his mum. • Peter wanted the toys and was angry that his mum said no. • Peter wanted his mum to feel guilty for not buying him the toy. Do not accept 'He was sent to his room'.	1
5	(2b)	Accept any reference to the following two obsessions listed in the text: • plastic spinners • football cards Do not accept general references to 'toys' or 'games'.	1
6	(2a)	Award 1 mark for reference to any of the following: • Nobody was really speaking to each other. • Everyone was cross so nobody spoke. • The mealtime was less lively than usual. • They would normally chat but today they didn't. Accept any other reference to the contrast between a normal mealtime and the more subdued version in the story, e.g. they weren't as happy as they usually are.	1
7	(2a)	Award 1 mark for a reference to any of the following: • The toys were thrown across the floor. • The toys hadn't been tidied away. • Peter didn't look after his toys very well. • The toys were just left where they'd been dropped. • There were a lot of toys in the room. • Peter had moved on to new things and left the old toys out. • Peter didn't appreciate the things he had. Do not accept reference to Peter throwing the toys down in anger, e.g. Peter threw the toys down because he couldn't have what he wanted.	1
8	(2b)	Award 1 mark for references to Peter feeling ashamed (for not remembering the boy's name). Do not accept references to Peter feeling dejected or full of self-pity.	1
9	(2d)	Award 1 mark for one of the following with a plausible justification. Award 2 marks for two of the following with plausible justifications. • It says 'she sighed', which indicates she felt fed-up/exasperated/sad/disappointed as he already had lots of toys. • She says, 'Oh Peter, if only you'd…', which suggests she is annoyed that he can't see sense/see her viewpoint. • The text says that she 'cleared the dishes in silence', which suggests she is angry and/or reflecting on Peter's behaviour.	Up to 2
10	(2a)	Award 1 mark for **Peter was seeing someone else's point of view for once.**	1
11	(2d)	Award 1 mark for what Peter will say and 1 mark for the reason, e.g. • Peter will apologise to his mum because he feels guilty for how he behaved. • Peter will say sorry to his mum for acting spoilt/being rude.	2
12	(2b)	Award 1 mark for any reference to Peter's mother, e.g. • Mum	1

Question (Content domain)		Requirement	Mark
13	*(2d)*	Both parts of the question need answering for 2 marks. 0 marks for a partly answered question. The answer must include that Peter realised how lucky/fortunate he was and that he will change by being more grateful for what he has got/not constantly asking for new things.	Up to 2
14	*(2a)*	Award 1 mark for both of the following: • (the) trend • fashionable (contrast) Do not accept 'popular'.	1
15	*(2b)*	Award 1 mark for reference to the First World War, e.g. 'The poor times during the war' or 'The wartime'.	1
16	*(2a)*	Award 1 mark for **high-tech**	1
17	*(2b)*	Award 1 mark for all four correct: Bellbottomed trousers were originally designed for the army. (FALSE) Frisbees are usually 20–25 cm in diameter. (TRUE) Cabbage Patch Kids were invented in the 1890s. (FALSE) The Frisbee craze hit the United States in the 1950s. (TRUE)	1
18	*(2b)*	Award 1 mark for each of the following up to a maximum of 2 marks: • Bellbottoms weren't available everywhere – people made their own. • Cabbage Patch Kids were in high demand – shops held lotteries to allocate the dolls. Accept any other reasonable explanation of a downside to a craze, along with an acceptable explanation of how it was dealt with or resolved.	Up to 2
19	*(2b)*	Award 1 mark for each of the following: • individual name • birth certificate	Up to 2
20	*(2a)*	Award 1 mark for **sky-rocketed**	1
21	*(2b)*	Award 1 mark for **1948**	1
22	*(2b)*	Award 1 mark for **USA** Also accept 'America'.	1
23	*(2d)*	Award 1 mark for **hysteria** Do not accept 'famous'.	1
24	*(2b)*	Award 1 mark for **49 days** Do not accept '49' without 'days'.	1
25	*(2d)*	Award 1 mark for all four correct: Kelly's first attempt lasted 13 hours and 13 minutes. (FACT) Alvin Kelly only did reckless things in his lifetime. (OPINION) 20,000 people watched Kelly in Atlantic City. (FACT) Flagpole sitting was the most unusual fad of the 20th century. (OPINION)	1
26	*(2c)*	Award 1 mark for **A brief history of crazes and fads through the decades.**	1
27	*(2f)*	Award 1 mark for all correctly matched: Toys – Details about some popular and successful playthings Fashion – The history and beginnings of fashions in clothing Just Crazy! – A description of one of the more unusual crazes from the past Fads, Crazes and Trends over Time – An overview and introduction	1
28	*(2d)*	Award 1 mark for reference to learning or improving knowledge of science. Do not accept references to being able to make money from selling the slime or it being fun to play with.	1
29	*(2d)*	Acceptable points: • It can be made using simple ingredients. • It's fun to play with. • It can be personalised. • There are opportunities in the commercial slime business. • It can help with concentration levels in class. • It's doing something creative. Award 2 marks for two acceptable points, with only one supported with evidence. Award 3 marks for two acceptable points, each supported with evidence, e.g. • 'You don't need any special ingredients to make it and if you made a lot of really good slime, you could sell it to your friends to make some money' • 'You could make it with your friends and have a party. It's good to make something fun and not spend all day looking at your phone' Award 2 marks for either two acceptable points, or one acceptable point supported with evidence, e.g. • 'It's fun because lots of people want to try it out' Award 1 mark for two acceptable points or one point supported by evidence, e.g. • 'You can put your own stuff in it'	Up to 3

Question (Content domain)		Requirement	Mark
30a	*(2d)*	Award 1 mark for any reference to her having made it before, or experimented with the ingredients, e.g. 'She has obviously made lots of different versions, some have worked out and some haven't' or 'She knows what she's talking about because she knows how to make all the different varieties'.	1
30b	*(2d)*	Award 1 mark for any of the following: • The mess she makes when she makes the slime • The use of the ingredients she needs • The amount of time she is spending Also accept quotations which make an acceptable point. Do not accept references to other people not liking the slime/it creating a problem at school/her selling the slime.	1
31	*(2d)*	Acceptable points: • Intelligent • Shrewd/astute • Business-like/money-orientated • Manipulative/cunning • Creative Award 2 marks for two acceptable points, with only one supported with evidence. Award 3 marks for two acceptable points, each supported with evidence, e.g. • 'She sort of tricks her friends into wanting the slime she has made by cleverly lending it to them so they want some of their own' • 'She makes people want what she's selling so she can make money' Award 2 marks for either two acceptable points, or one acceptable point with evidence, e.g. • 'She's good at selling her slime. She makes it herself' • 'She makes lots of the slime herself, and it was her idea to sell it' Award 1 mark for two acceptable points or one acceptable point supported with evidence, e.g. • 'She thought selling it would be a good idea' • 'She's clever' Do not accept general responses about Matilda being nice/a good friend, etc.	Up to 3
32	*(2d)*	Award 1 mark for any two of the following: • astutely • spotted a gap in the market • marketing ploy • maximise sales • 'try before they buy'	1
33	*(2d)*	Award 1 mark for **At first she loved the idea, but then it became an issue.**	1
34	*(2b)*	Award 1 mark for reference to both things, and 1 mark for the reason: • Amanda must clean the table and floors because they often have slime on them.	Up to 2
35	*(2g)*	Award 1 mark for reference to either of the following: • People will be fanatical about it. • Everyone will want it. or • It is aimed at children. • Adults are getting fed up of crazes. or • It's one craze amongst many. • It's another craze to follow others.	1
36	*(2d)*	Award 1 mark for **safe to use.**	1
37	*(2a)*	Award 1 mark for: Ready-made slime **makers**	1
		Award 1 mark for: are scrambling to be the **most visible**	1
38	*(2b)*	Award 1 mark for all four correct: Slime can be made from glue. (TRUE) Borax is also known as sodium borate. (TRUE) Adults are all opposed to slime. (FALSE) Slime can be personalised. (TRUE)	1

Set A English grammar, punctuation and spelling – Paper 1: questions

Content domain coverage for the questions in this paper are shown in the table of answers below. Information about these codes can be found in the KS2 English Grammar, Punctuation and Spelling test framework.

Question (Content domain)	Requirement	Mark
1 (G6.3)	Award 1 mark for all three correct. **Word:** fear, read, slow — **Suffix:** able, ly, less (fear→less, read→able, slow→ly)	1
2 (G1.8)	Award 1 mark for all three correct. **Sentence / Determiner:** At the supermarket, I bought _____ peaches. → some; I also bought _____ avocado. → an; I carried all _____ shopping home. → the	1
3 (G1.9)	Award 1 mark for the correct word circled. My mother brought a (snack) for me after school. or My mother brought (a snack) for me after school.	1
4 (G3.3)	Award 1 mark for three conjunctions inserted correctly. We should bring coats **and** umbrellas **if** the weather looks poor, **but** we should also bring sun cream just in case!	1
5 (G5.3)	Award 1 mark for **Shall I play with Jake today**	1
6 (G1.6)	Award 1 mark for the correct insertion of an appropriate adverb, e.g. He slammed the car door **angrily**. He slammed the car door **hurriedly**. He slammed the car door **quickly**. He slammed the car door **hastily**. Do not accept misspellings of the adverb.	1
7 (G5.10)	Award 1 mark for **I needed several ingredients: some flour, two eggs, sugar and a vanilla pod.**	1
8 (G5.7)	Award 1 mark for all four inverted commas in the correct place: 'When we have finished our writing,' said the teacher, 'we will start a new topic.'	1
9 (G5.6b)	Award 1 mark for a correctly placed comma. Glancing behind her**,** the girl continued down the street.	1
10 (G1.5)	Award 1 mark for the correct pronouns: When the children had finished playing, **they** tidied away all the toys. Dad was so impressed with the tidy room, **he** gave all the children a treat.	1
11 (G4.1d)	Award 1 mark for a correctly completed table.	1
12 (G5.13)	Award 1 mark for **The kind-hearted girl raised money for charity.**	1
13 (G4.1c)	Award 1 mark for **I won't be available to help.**	1
14 (G2.1)	Award 1 mark for all four correct.	1

Question 11 table:

Sentence	Present progressive	Past progressive
Sara is getting excited about the birthday party.	✓	
Sara was talking about which present to choose.		✓
Sara is preparing a surprise for her friend.	✓	

Question 14 table:

Sentence	Function
What a coincidence it was	exclamation
Did you enjoy the trip to the theatre	question
There were 20 people at the park	statement
Put the bags down and come inside	command

Question (Content domain)	Requirement	Mark
15 (G7.1)	Award 1 mark for **I travelled to France to visit my sister.**	1
16 (G5.8)	Award 1 mark for the correct expanded form inserted into each box. **She will** call round when **we have** eaten dinner. I **do not** know why.	1
17 (G5.9)	a) Award 1 mark for the correct response. Brackets / a pair of brackets	1
	b) Award 1 mark for the correct response. Commas / a pair of commas or Dashes / a pair of dashes	1
18 (G5.4)	Award 1 mark for two correct sentences ticked. The sentence should end with a full stop instead of an exclamation mark. There should be a question mark after the word pencil.	1
19 (G5.1)	Award 1 mark for **In April, my cousin will fly from London to Rome for a holiday.**	1
20 (G5.11)	Award 1 mark for semi-colon in correct place: My friends are going shopping**;** they need new uniform for school.	1
21 (G5.8)	Award 1 mark for word correctly circled: I can't seem to find (Claire's) phone number and I'm supposed to call her later on.	1
22 (G6.4)	Award 1 mark for **small**	1
23 (G5.5)	Award 1 mark for a correctly completed table.	1

Sentence	Commas used correctly	Commas used incorrectly
We should buy some cheese, bread and a box of eggs.	✓	
They ran all, over the field looking for their lost dog.		✓
My wallet, old and worn, is never very full of money.	✓	
She looked at the clock and, realised she was late.		✓

Question (Content domain)	Requirement	Mark
24 (G1.7)	Award 1 mark for both words circled. They ran (under) the bridge and hid (behind) a large bush.	1
25 (G2.2)	Award 1 mark for the correct response. Was he talking to the police?	1
26 (G4.2)	Award 1 mark for both words circled. He (bit) into his sandwich just as the train (came) into the station.	1
27 (G3.4)	Award 1 mark for an understanding that the subordinate clause has the purpose of explaining why Sam would not go into the water.	1
28 (G1.4)	Award 1 mark for both words circled. Put the kitten down (before) you drop her. I hung out all the washing, (although) the rain clouds were darkening.	1
29 (G3.1)	Award 1 mark for a correctly completed table.	1

	Main clause	Subordinate clause
The light was fading <u>because it was nearly evening time</u>.		✓
The kettle, <u>which was brand new</u>, began to boil.		✓
When the clock struck twelve, <u>my tummy began to rumble</u>.	✓	

Question (Content domain)	Requirement	Mark
30 (G5.6a)	a) Award 1 mark for a correctly placed comma. Once they had asked Mum, Joe and Kate went bowling.	1
	b) Award 1 mark for correctly placed commas. Once they had asked, Mum, Joe and Kate went bowling. Do not accept the use of a serial comma. Once they had asked, Mum, Joe, and Kate went bowling.	1

Question (Content domain)	Requirement	Mark
31 (G1.4)	Award 1 mark for both words circled. The puppy wagged his tail furiously, (but) Jack took no notice (and) went inside the house.	1
32 (G6.2)	Award 1 mark for an explanation of both sentences, e.g. The customer complained that the chicken was uncooked. *This means that the chicken was raw.* *This means that the chicken was not cooked at all.* The customer complained that the chicken was overcooked. *This means that the chicken has been cooked for too long.*	1
33 (G1.5a)	Award 1 mark for the correct possessive pronoun inserted into each sentence. That doll belongs to my sister. The doll is **hers**. The car belongs to them. The car is **theirs**. The keys belong to us. They keys are **ours**. Do not accept a misspelling of the word 'theirs'.	1
34 (G6.1)	a) Award 1 mark for a correct explanation of the word synonym, e.g. They are words that have the same meaning.	1

	b) Award 1 mark for a word that is a synonym of the word frightened, e.g.
	    • terrified
	    • scared
		1

35 (G4.1a)	Award 1 mark for all three correct. Last Tuesday, the family **went** out for a walk. They **walked** through some woods and **saw** lots of wildlife. Do not accept misspellings of verb forms.	1
36 (G1.3)	Award 1 mark for two correct adjectives derived from the given nouns, e.g. Even though she felt **nervous**, Chloe reached out to touch the unicorn's **beautiful** mane. It was a **magical** experience. Do not accept misspellings of the adjectives.	1
37 (G1.5b)	Award 1 mark for **who's**	1
38 (G1.2)	Award 1 mark for a grammatically correct sentence that uses wish as a verb and that is correctly punctuated, e.g. I wish I could have a pony of my own. Do not accept responses that use an inflected ending of wish, e.g. Sara wished she had more friends.	1
(G1.1)	Award 1 mark for a grammatically correct sentence that uses wish as a noun and that is correctly punctuated, e.g. I made a wish as I blew out the candle. Do not accept responses that use an inflected ending of wish, e.g. The children signed the card with best wishes.	1
39 (G3.1a)	Award 1 mark for the full relative clause underlined. The new car <u>which is parked on our driveway</u> is in need of a wash.	1
40 (G4.4)	Award 1 mark for a correctly completed table.	1

Sentence	Active	Passive
The chocolate bar was melted by the sun.		✓
The children washed the windows.	✓	
The candles were blown out by the boy.		✓

Question (Content domain)	Requirement	Mark
41 (G1.6)	Award 1 mark for both words circled. The children were playing (noisily,) so I had to step (outside.)	1
42 (G4.4)	Award 1 mark for a correctly punctuated sentence using the active voice. *The judge sentenced the prisoner.*	1
43 (G3.2)	Award 1 mark for **as an expanded noun phrase**	1
44 (G4.3)	Award 1 mark for **were**	1
45 (G4.1b)	Award 1 mark for an indication that the present perfect form uses the words 'has finished' to show that now the homework is complete.	1
46 (G5.4)	Award 1 mark for an indication that the full stop can be replaced with an exclamation mark. '!'	1

Set A English grammar, punctuation and spelling – Paper 2: spelling

1. The word is **misunderstanding**.
There has been some kind of *misunderstanding*.
The word is **misunderstanding**.

2. The word is **known**.
I have *known* my best friend for many years.
The word is **known**.

3. The word is **recorded**.
He secretly *recorded* the conversation.
The word is **recorded**.

4. The word is **sensible**.
Sam is the most *sensible* person I know.
The word is **sensible**.

5. The word is **preferred**.
He *preferred* fruit to vegetables.
The word is **preferred**.

6. The word is **conclusion**.
I came to a startling *conclusion*.
The word is **conclusion**.

7. The word is **undervalued**.
I fear the house has been *undervalued*.
The word is **undervalued**.

8. The word is **difference**.
There is a huge *difference* in clothes sizes.
The word is **difference**.

9. The word is **currency**.
We must remember to buy *currency* for the holiday.
The word is **currency**.

10. The word is **though**.
Even *though* I was afraid, I stood up to speak.
The word is **though**.

11. The word is **quay**.
The ships were docked at the *quay*.
The word is **quay**.

12. The word is **devious**.
The *devious* king was not popular among his subjects.
The word is **devious**.

13. The word is **religious**.
Most children have *religious* education at school.
The word is **religious**.

14. The word is **magician**.
The *magician* captivated the young children.
The word is **magician**.

15. The word is **torrential**.
The *torrential* rain lasted for several hours.
The word is **torrential**.

16. The word is **weightlessness**.
Astronauts experience *weightlessness* in space.
The word is **weightlessness**.

17. The word is **forgetting**.
I keep *forgetting* where I've put my keys.
The word is **forgetting**.

18. The word is **receipt**.
Keep the *receipt* in case you need to return it.
The word is **receipt**.

19. The word is **competition**.
I won a prize in the *competition*.
The word is **competition**.

20. The word is **viciously**.
The dog *viciously* attacked the new toy.
The word is **viciously**.

Set B Reading

Content domain coverage for the questions in this paper are shown in the table of answers below. Information about these codes can be found in the KS2 English Reading test framework.

Question (Content domain)		Requirement	Mark
1	(2a)	Award 1 mark for **boulders** Do not accept stone.	1
2	(2a)	Award 1 mark for **impressive**	1
3	(2g)	Award 1 mark for reference to any of the following, up to a maximum of 2 marks: • The lakes looked like they were dug out of the ground. • The rivers were quiet/slow and gentle. • The rivers wound around.	Up to 2
4	(2b)	Award 1 mark for recognition that Finn realises Benandonner was much bigger than he had realised e.g. *Benandonner was a great deal bigger than he had previously thought* Also accept reference to Finn's response to seeing the giant, e.g. • Recognition that Finn is in a hurry to get away: *he quickly scrambled home* • Recognition that Finn realises he's made a mistake: *he'd stupidly challenged Benandonner to a fight but realised he probably shouldn't have*	1
5	(2d)	Two separate things must be identified to gain the available mark. These should include the following: • Quickly scrambling home when he realised that Benandonner was bigger than him. (This answer point must include **scrambling home**, not just the realisation of the size difference.) • Finn beginning to shake when Benandonner knocked on his door.	1
6	(2d)	Award 1 mark for reference to any two of the following: • brave • intelligent • quick-thinking • smarter than the giant • inventive Do not accept inaccurate conceptions, e.g. she is a mother.	1
7	(2b)	Award 1 mark for reference to any of the following (whether given as acceptable point or quotation), up to a maximum of 3 marks: • showed him a tree and said it was a spear • showed him a block of wood and said it was a shield • cooked him cake with stones in • pretended Finn was the baby • gave him a drink which made him confused • showed him boulders Finn used to 'play catch' Accept quotations that meet an acceptable point. Longer quotations that cover more than one acceptable point should be awarded 1 mark.	Up to 3
8	(2b)	Award 1 mark for **Overconfident**	1
9a	(2b)	Accept one mark for any of the following: • He struggled to lift the boulder. • He couldn't play with the boulders like Finn.	1
9b	(2b)	Award 1 mark for references to either his only hurting himself a little or that he had good sense, e.g. 'he hurt himself a little' 'luckily he was a tough giant'	1
10	(2b)	Award 1 mark for **The Isle of Man**	1
11	(2b)	Award 1 mark for three correct. Award 2 marks for all four correct: Finn felt great affection for the Scottish giant. (FALSE) Finn built the causeway to make friends with the Scottish giant. (FALSE) Finn was married. (TRUE) Finn underestimated the size of the Scottish giant. (TRUE)	Up to 2
12a	(2b)	Award 1 mark for **summer.**	1
12b	(2b)	Award 1 mark for **fighting with another boy.**	1
12c	(2b)	Award 1 mark for **told them off, gave them a clip around the ear and sent them to bed.**	1
12d	(2b)	Award 1 mark for **bravely checked the chest of drawers.**	1

Question (Content domain)		Requirement	Mark
13	(2d)	Award 1 mark for a reference to either of the following: • Dad sent the boys to bed early or • the reference to 'too early – and too light – to try to go to sleep' suggesting they wouldn't normally have gone to bed yet	1
14	(2d)	Award 2 marks for answers which refer to Dad's temperament or character and the inference that he has lashed out before, e.g. • Dad has a quick temper and has hit the boys in the past. • The boys know that Dad might hit them if they don't behave because he's done it in the past. Award 1 mark for responses that either explain Dad's temper/violence or the fact he has been violent in the past, e.g. • Dad's clipped them before. • They know he'll get angry.	Up to 2
15	(2b)	Award 1 mark for both correct: • The boys sat side by side and chatted. • The boys huddled together when they saw the ghost.	1

16a	(2d)	Award 1 mark for reference to each of the following up to a maximum of 2 marks:
		• That they hid from the ghost:
		  – shuffled quickly under the bed
		
		• That they couldn't move with fear:
		  – …but just sat as still as statues
		  – We were rigid with shock
		  – I think we were in shock
		  – …in pure fear
		
		Do not accept references to the boys questioning each other about what they saw, or checking the curtains and chest of drawers the following morning.
			Up to 2

16b	(2d)	Award 1 mark for reference to any of the following: • the boys reassuring each other it was a shadow or bedclothes • the boys reassuring each other that they must have imagined it Do not accept reference to it being a new day/as if nothing had happened.	1
17	(2d)	Award 1 mark for reference to any of the following, up to a maximum of 2 marks: • lived in a rough street • lived in a poor part of town • the furniture had been passed down (chest of drawers) • thin curtains • cheap blankets • shabby carpet • sharing a bedroom • old metal beds • old furniture • little terraced house Accept quotations that meet an acceptable point.	Up to 2
18	(2d)	Award 1 mark for reference to one of the following: • the intense rivalry between Cunard and the White Star Line • the desire to build bigger and faster ships • the company wanting to make as much money as possible	1
19	(2d)	Award 1 mark for an answer referring to the size of the job (or the size of the ship) and completing the work to a high standard.	1
20	(2b)	Award 1 mark for an answer referring to either or both of the following: • just off the coast of Newfoundland • in the North Atlantic	1

Question (Content domain)	Requirement	Mark
21 (2e)	Acceptable points (yes): • They might build smaller, more manageable ships in the future. • They might have ensured that there were enough lifeboat places. • They might have made sure everyone attended the safety practices. • They might have avoided areas where there might be icebergs. Acceptable points (no): • They would still want to be the best shipping line in the world. • They would not have added any more lifeboats. • They would try to build an even bigger ship. • They would try to make even more money from having even more passengers on board. Award 3 marks for three acceptable points or two acceptable points with at least one supported with evidence, e.g. • They might have decided to have enough lifeboat seats for everyone and made sure everyone knew how to get off the boat safely. The ship was too big really, so they could build smaller ones next time. • Even though the *Titanic* sank, they would probably still want to be the best in the world and build even bigger boats to carry more passengers because it said that there was a big rivalry. Award 2 marks for two acceptable points or one acceptable point supported with evidence, e.g. • They would probably put more lifeboats on board and have a safety drill every day, just in case. • They might stay away from the icebergs in future because they were going fast and it was hard to avoid them in time. Award 1 mark for one acceptable point, e.g. • Yes, they might put safety notices up. • No, they would still want to be called the best. Do not accept answer which speculates about points not mentioned in the acceptable points list.	Up to 3
22 (2d)	Acceptable points refer to: • the prestige of being on board with a lot of dignitaries • the extremely high standards on board • the quite low price of a third class ticket • the chance to travel on the biggest ship ever built • the chance to go to America • being able to say that you were on the first voyage of the *Titanic* Also accept answers which refer to the thrill of going somewhere new, or travelling on a great ship. Do not accept answers which only reference going away, or travelling without including details about the special nature of the ship. Award 3 marks for three acceptable points or two acceptable points, with at least one supported with evidence, e.g. • People would want to rub shoulders with lords and ladies on the biggest ship in the world. The price of a ticket wasn't really that much to be able to do that. • They would travel on the biggest ship in the world to America and they would have a great time on board too because they had lots to do. Award 2 marks for two acceptable points or one acceptable point supported with evidence, e.g. • They would like to say that they had been there on the first voyage and travelled to America. • They would enjoy the journey because the standards were a lot higher than people were used to. Award 1 mark for identifying one acceptable point, e.g. • The rooms were nice. • There were famous people on board.	Up to 3
23 (2f)	Award 1 mark for all correctly matched: | Before the building began	Despite the many technical and safety questions raised, *Titanic*'s demise is an example of the power of nature and mankind's over-reliance on technology.
During the building process	There were some occasional warnings of ice from other ships, but the sea was calm and she was sailing well so there seemed to be no reason for alarm.
During the voyage	The hull was towed to a huge fitting out dock, where thousands of workers spent the next year building her decks and completing the fittings to the highest possible standard.
After the tragedy	Cunard and the White Star Line were striving to outdo each other.		1

Question (Content domain)		Requirement	Mark
24	(2d)	Award 1 mark for answers referring to either the relatively cheap cost of the ticket or the smaller amount of space required for third class accommodation compared to other classes, e.g. • It was a cheap ticket to get them across the world. • Third class rooms were smaller so there was space for more of them. Also accept answers which refer to a new start in life, or the chance to sail on a big, new ship. Do not accept answers which refer to there being more third class tickets than any other kind.	1
25	(2d)	Award 1 mark for reference to any of the following: • The ship was bigger than they may have imagined. • The ship was more luxurious than they perhaps expected. • Their second class rooms were like first class on any other ship. Do not accept reference to their having to do less work because of the staff or crew on board the ship.	1
26	(2a)	Award 1 mark for any of: • not completely without hindrance • hindrance • a small coal fire in a bunker • near collision • a bad omen	1
27a	(2b)	Award 1 mark for reference to two of the following: • Some feared the hull was simply too big. • There was a small fire on board before she sailed. • There was a near miss with another ship as *Titanic* left the dock.	1
27b	(2b)	Award 1 mark for both of the following correctly identified: • called for help • ordered the lifeboats to be filled and lowered.	1
28	(2a)	Award 1 mark for **disorganised**	1
29	(2a)	Award 1 mark for reference to any of the following: • She begged them to help the others. • She was pleading for them to turn around. • She was trying not to demand it but really wanted it to happen. Also accept reference to how Molly may have been feeling about those left behind, e.g. Molly may have had family left behind.	1
30	(2b)	Award 1 mark for **John Jacob Astor IV**	1
31	(2a)	Award 1 mark for references which include any of the following: • avoided • went around • tried to miss	1
32	(2a)	Award 1 mark for **unable to conquer the elements**	1
33	(2c)	Award 1 mark for the correct sequence: The aftermath **6** Opposition and rivalry **1** Construction commences **2** Alarm bells and damages **4** Sinking of the ship **3** Chaotic evacuation **5**	1

Set B English grammar, punctuation and spelling – Paper 1: questions

Content domain coverage for the questions in this paper are shown in the table of answers below. Information about these codes can be found in the KS2 English Grammar, Punctuation and Spelling test framework.

Question (Content domain)	Requirement	Mark
1 (G2.2)	Award 1 mark for **At what point did you give up**	1
2 (G5.11)	Award 1 mark for a correctly placed semi-colon: Go and visit your grandmother; she is expecting you.	1
3 (G1.5)	Award 1 mark for an indication that the use of the pronoun ('he') avoids repetition of the name 'Harry'.	1
4 (G6.2)	Award 1 mark for **To force out of position.**	1
5 (G4.1b)	Award 1 mark for **was washing**	1
6 (G7.1)	Award 1 mark for the correct words circled. The streamers and balloons (was/**were**) very brightly-coloured. The first time I saw tigers and lions (**was**/were) at the zoo. My cousins (was/**were**) excited about visiting in the holidays.	1
7 (G5.6b)	Award 1 mark for **Without hesitation, Miles accepted the offer of a place at the university.**	1
8 (G5.5)	Award 1 mark for **Noah brushed his teeth, put on his pyjamas, turned out his lamp and went to sleep.**	1
9 (G1.6)	Award 1 mark for **adverb**	1
10 (G5.10)	Award 1 mark for colon in correct place: I have four best friends: Tom (my brother), Sam, James and Nathan.	1
11 (G1.8)	Award 1 mark for **determiners**	1
12 (G5.12)	Award 1 mark for **I love going swimming – it's a great way to keep fit.**	1
13 (G1.3)	Award 1 mark for **Ben had a firm grip on the trophy.**	1
14 (G5.9)	Award 1 mark for **The flask holds 1 litre (1000 millilitres) of liquid.**	1
15 (G1.6)	Award 1 mark for an explanation that indicates an understanding that an adverb modifies (accept 'changes') a verb (also accept adjective or adverb if they are in addition to the word 'verb').	1
16 (G1.4)	Award 1 mark for the correct insertion of an appropriate subordinating conjunction, e.g. We stopped off for a drink **because** it was a hot day. We stopped off for a drink **as** it was a hot day. We stopped off for a drink **since** it was a hot day.	1
17 (G2.4)	Award 1 mark for **What a lot of pizza you have eaten**	1
18 (G1.2)	Award 1 mark for **I began to chip at the dried plaster.**	1
19 (G1.7)	Award 1 mark for the inclusion of a preposition indicating an understanding of this type of word to express *when* the child was looking carefully, e.g. *before* or *while* crossing the road.	1
20 (G1.5)	Award 1 mark for correctly placed pronouns: Sarah asked her parents for some pocket money but **they** asked **her** to clean out the rabbit hutch first.	1
21 (G5.7)	Award 1 mark for **The teacher asked, "Who owns this bag?"**	1
22 (G7.3)	Award 1 mark for **You are cordially invited to a party.**	1
23 (G3.4)	Award 1 mark for **The class, <u>which is mainly boys</u>, loves science lessons.**	1
24 (G6.1)	Award 1 mark for correct circling. Despite the twins appearing to be (identical) they are actually (different) in many ways.	1
25 (G5.8)	Award 1 mark for a correctly completed table.	1

	Apostrophe for omission	Apostrophe for possession
My mother's friend is called Tina.		✓
We're going away tomorrow.	✓	
The dog's collar is broken.		✓
She's bringing some cakes tomorrow.	✓	

Question (Content domain)	Requirement	Mark
26 *(G3.1a)*	Award 1 mark for **A girl who I know from school is coming to karate class.**	1
27 *(G2.1)*	Award 1 mark for **I will pack a picnic for everyone to share**	1
28 *(G5.2)*	Award 1 mark for capital letters and full stops correctly inserted. Jane picked up the full rubbish bag. She carried it to the bin. She opened the lid but an enormous split appeared in the bag. There was rubbish all over the floor.	1
29 *(G5.6a)*	Award 1 mark for a correctly placed pair of commas. The team, which was made up of children at my school, won the match easily.	1
30 *(G4.2)*	Award 1 mark for any correct choice of tense for both verbs. For example, The mice **nibbled** at the corner of the box of cat food. Josh **spoke** very softly when he gave his reasons for leaving.	1
31 *(G2.3)*	Award 1 mark for a grammatically correct and accurately punctuated command that uses an imperative, e.g. *Put toothpaste on the brush.* *Take out your toothbrush.* *Brush your teeth!*	1
32 *(G3.1)*	Award 1 mark for all three correct. As the book was so interesting (S), I found myself reading it often (M) and offered to share it with the class (M).	1
33 *(G1.4)*	Award 1 mark for all three correct. They bought new running shoes (when) the sale was on. (Although) the weather was poor, they were determined to cross the finish line. The race went extremely well, (so) they decided to sign up for another.	1
34 *(G1.7)*	Award 1 mark for both: **The tortoise moved very slowly towards the lettuce.** **My cat walked carefully along the garden fence.**	1
35 *(G1.9)*	Award 1 mark for John	1
36 *(G1.4)*	Award 1 mark for a grammatically correct sentence, which includes a conjunction indicating an understanding of this type of word to express cause, such as 'because', 'so', e.g. I am hungry **because** I forgot to have breakfast. She was late **so** she missed the bus.	1
37 *(G1.5b)*	Award 1 mark for the correct word circled. My mother sent me an enormous fruit basket, (which) contained bananas, grapes, cherries and a mango.	1
38 *(G4.1a)*	Award 1 mark for all three correct. I **took** my car to a mechanic yesterday to have it **repaired** but I **was** not prepared for the cost! Do not accept misspellings of verb forms.	1
39 *(G5.9)*	Award 1 mark for a correctly placed pair of brackets The most populated city in the world is Tokyo **(**population 37,833,000**)** in Japan.	1
40 *(G6.2)* *(G6.1)*	Award 1 mark for the correct prefix: un	1
41 *(G6.1)*	Award 1 mark for both synonyms circled. The (stories) written by Roald Dahl are popular with children and adults around the world. His (tales) are captivating and yet sometimes a little dark.	1
42 *(G1.5a)*	Award 1 mark for the correct word circled. I was completely surprised that Sam didn't only eat Amara's ice cream but ate (yours) as well.	1
43 *(G5.11)*	Award 1 mark for **semi-colon**	1
44 *(G6.3)*	Award 1 mark for two correct words derived from the word care, e.g. He **carelessly** dropped litter all over the park. He was always **caring** for stray animals he found in the village. Do not accept misspellings.	1
45 *(G1.1)*	Award 1 mark for the correct noun inserted. She always found badminton to be a source of great **enjoyment**. Do not accept misspellings of enjoyment.	1
46 *(G5.13)*	Award 1 mark for two correctly placed hyphens. On the way home, I could tell the children were **over-tired**, which they demonstrated in a very **bad-tempered** way.	1

Question (Content domain)	Requirement	Mark
47 (G4.4)	Award 1 mark for a correctly punctuated sentence using the active. The babysitter put the exhausted children to bed.	1
48 (G4.1d)	Award 1 mark for both correct. Judy **is baking** cakes. She **is hoping** to sell them to her friends on Monday. Do not accept misspellings of verb forms.	1
49 (G3.2)	Award 1 mark for an appropriate noun phrase of three or more words inserted into the sentence, e.g. The landscape gardener was working hard in the garden. My wonderful father was working hard in the garden. The young boy was working hard in the garden.	1
50 (G1.6)	Award 1 mark for the correct word circled. You should think (hard) about your options before making such an untimely intervention.	1

Set B English grammar, punctuation and spelling – Paper 2: spelling

Instructions

Read the following instruction out to the child(ren).

I am going to read 20 sentences to you. Each sentence has a word missing. Listen carefully to the missing word and fill this in the answer space, making sure that you spell it correctly. I will read the word, then the word within a sentence, then repeat the word a third time.

You should now read the spellings three times, as given below. Leave at least a 12-second gap between spellings. At the end, read all the sentences again, giving the child(ren) the chance to make any changes they wish to their answers.

1. The word is **happily**.
They played *happily* together for hours.
The word is **happily**.

2. The word is **caught**.
I *caught* a cold that lasted for a week.
The word is **caught**.

3. The word is **nation**.
Trade with other countries brings jobs and wealth to our *nation*.
The word is **nation**.

4. The word is **obvious**.
It is *obvious* to me when you are lying.
The word is **obvious**.

5. The word is **design**.
She put a great deal of work into her *design*.
The word is **design**.

6. The word is **incredible**.
They found the stories of her adventures quite *incredible*.
The word is **incredible**.

7. The word is **confusing**.
The new way of organising the paperwork is quite *confusing*.
The word is **confusing**.

8. The word is **emergency**.
I know how to dial 999 in the event of an *emergency*.
The word is **emergency**.

9. The word is **compassion**.
He demonstrated real *compassion* for the refugees.
The word is **compassion**.

10. The word is **roughest**.
The sailor looked out at the *roughest* sea he had ever encountered.
The word is **roughest**.

11. The word is **thistle**.
Things were going well until she was scratched by a *thistle* in the grass.
The word is **thistle**.

12. The word is **probably**.
This is *probably* the longest I have ever spent at my desk.
The word is **probably**.

13. The word is **vacancy**.
The hotel manager advertised a *vacancy* for a receptionist.
The word is **vacancy**.

14. The word is **understanding**.
He was a very *understanding* and patient parent.
The word is **understanding**.

15. The word is **troubling**.
Something is *troubling* him, but I'm not sure what it is.
The word is **troubling**.

16. The word is **chemist**.
I must pop into the *chemist* for cough medicine on the way home.
The word is **chemist**.

17. The word is **myths**.
My favourite stories are *myths* and legends.
The word is **myths**.

18. The word is **amazingly**.
Amazingly, everyone got on with each other all day.
The word is **amazingly**.

19. The word is **solution**.
The boys worked all morning on a *solution* to the maths problem.
The word is **solution**.

20. The word is **cheque**.
Grandma said she is sending me a *cheque* for my birthday.
The word is **cheque**.

All the Wonderful Things

Mad Fad Memorabilia

Put the Spinners Down, Slime is Here!

Reading Booklet

Key Stage 2 English Reading Booklet – Set A

Contents

All the Wonderful Things

Peter whined and complained all the way home after school. He complained about having to wear his raincoat (too tight), he complained about having to walk through puddles (too dirty), he complained about his day (too boring) but most of all, he complained about how his friends all had Pickeez and he didn't.

Pickeez were the latest craze to sweep through the school. They were small, colourful plastic characters which came with a special collector card. Everyone in Peter's class had a collection already. George had twenty AND a rare golden Pickeez. They were the best ones to get. If you came to school holding a golden Pickeez, everyone wanted to see it. Peter thought George was a spoilt show-off and walked away every time he came close.

Peter's mother listened to his complaints and sighed. She thought about the boxes and boxes of toys in his room – all the crazes and fads he'd absolutely 'had to have'. After what felt like five minutes of obsession with a set of football cards or a plastic spinner, he'd get fed up and move on to the next 'big' thing. She felt sad that Peter seemed to feel he was being badly treated simply because she refused to buy yet more little plastic toys which would surely only end up the way of all the others – either stuffed in a box, under his bed or strewn across his bedroom floor.

Once home, Peter sulked in his room until dinner time. When his mum called him down to eat, he made a lot of exaggerated sighs and huffs, slid off the bed where he had been lying and stomped down the stairs.

After a very subdued meal, Peter's mother asked him to help tidy up the dishes.

"Why can't Charlie do it?" he demanded.

"Because Charlie is only one and he can't walk yet. He'd find it very difficult to carry things to the sink!" Mum replied.

"If I do it, will you buy me some Pickeez?"

"Oh Peter, if only you'd…"

But Peter cut across her, shouting "FORGET IT!" as he slammed the dishes down and stormed back to his room.

Mum chose to ignore Peter's outburst, and cleared the dishes in silence, with only Charlie's cooing and babbling for company.

Peter found getting through the next day at school extremely hard. He felt jealous and angry whenever he saw anyone with some Pickeez in their hands. He avoided all his friends at break time as they compared and boasted about their latest Pickeez acquisitions.

Peter found a quiet spot on a bench in the corner of the yard and sat down, dejected and full of self-pity. After a few moments, he realised someone else had come to sit next to him. Looking up, he saw it was the new boy in their class. Peter felt a little ashamed that he couldn't remember the boy's name.

"Hello Peter, I'm Mohammed," said the boy.

Peter remembered his mum telling him about the newcomers to the school – some children of a refugee family who had travelled a long way, through many dangers, to safety in this country. Peter decided to ask Mohammed to his house for tea.

Once the arrangements had been made by their respective parents, the boys walked back to Peter's house together. As soon as they'd hung up their coats and peeled off their shoes, they ran upstairs to Peter's room to play. Peter threw himself down on the floor to play with his Lego. Mohammed took in the room around him, crammed with boxes of toys, bookshelves full of books and piles of computer games in dusty heaps around the room.

"What's up?" said Peter.

"You have so much stuff! What a mess!" laughed Mohammed, picking up a forgotten pile of football cards from last season which Peter had badgered and begged for. "How do you ever find anything?"

Peter looked around his room and slowly took in all the wonderful things in it. He thought about all the times he had begged and demanded things from his mother, making her feel bad if she dared to say no to him. He considered the situation his new friend was in, all the terrible things he must have seen and how he had fled his own country with little more than a small bagful of belongings.

Suddenly, Peter realised something….

MAD FAD MEMORABILIA

Fads, Crazes and Trends over Time

There have been many fads over the years, some more mad than others. From flappers and flagpole sitting in the 1920s to dance marathons and zoot suits in the 1930s, fads and crazes have always had a place in life.

From the 1950s onwards, crazes really took off with the invention of the hula hoop and later, the adoption of bellbottomed trousers and towering platform shoes, lava lamps and mysterious mood rings. The 1980s and 1990s were just as prolific with the frustration of the Rubik's Cube, the dawn of Beanie Babies and the fascination with MySpace.

More recent fads include planking, selfies and fidget spinners. It's impossible to tell what will be next. Who knows what our future fads will be?

Here, we take a whistle-stop look at fads in fashion, fads in kids' toys, and fads that are just plain crazy!

Read on to find out more about some of the more unusual fads from modern history.

Fashion

Maybe more than any other type of fad, fashions often have a short-term – but striking – impact.

Bellbottoms

Bellbottomed trousers became a fashion staple of hip and happening society in the late 1960s and early 1970s.

Bellbottoms are trousers that flare widely at the bottom. They were originally designed for the navy, with the loose bottom of the trouser ensuring that sailors could quickly remove their boots when needed.

They were usually made from denim and were incredibly popular. They were not, however, available everywhere so some creative fashion-followers adapted their own, standard jeans by cutting the leg seam and adding a triangular panel of different fabric.

When popular celebrities of the day such as Elvis Presley began to wear this style of trouser, the trend was quickly taken up by young people, who viewed them as a fashionable contrast to the straight-legged and more conservative trousers worn by the older generation.

Click here to continue

Leisure Suits

A leisure suit is a casual suit, usually associated with the suit style of the 1970s. But the introduction of a trousers-and-jacket set that was more comfortable and intended for casual occasions, or no occasion at all, actually came well before the disco era.

A 'lounge suit' can be traced back to the mid-1800s in Britain. This was basically a less-structured, more casual daytime suit, where the jacket and trousers were made from different fabrics.

The more modern leisure suit dates back to the 1920s, following the austerity of the First World War. The roaring '20s brought a much more youthful look and feel, with women in boyish 'flapper' attire and men in loose-fitting suits that were sometimes known as 'sack suits'.

In the 1950s, and with the introduction of a new clothing fabric called polyester, the leisure suit really began to take off. By the 1970s, it was the staple costume of any self-respecting disco dude, often with bellbottomed trousers, pastel colours and occasionally a pattern.

They were a short-term fashion – by the 1980s, the suits had almost entirely lost their appeal.

Toys

From a simple hoop or ball and cup in Victorian times, to high-tech virtual reality headsets today, the ways children are entertained and amused has changed enormously over the centuries.

Cabbage Patch Kids

In the 1980s, Cabbage Patch Kids became one of the hugest toy success stories of the decade. With their chubby faces, squashy arms and tiny, close-set eyes, the dolls were a dramatic departure from the run-of-the-mill sweet baby doll. The manufacturing process meant that each Cabbage Patch Kid was very slightly different from every other one.

Originally the invention of 21-year-old Xavier Roberts, a sculptor, the dolls were created as part of an art exhibit. Roberts got his assistants to present the dolls for 'adoption' rather than for sale, each doll coming with its own individual name and birth certificate. This unusual approach to marketing worked, as sales across the world sky-rocketed.

At the height of their popularity, such was demand for the dolls that shops had to hold lotteries to choose people at random who could buy them. Sales grew dramatically from $60 million in their first year to more than $600 million in 1985.

Click here to continue

Frisbees

The ever-popular Frisbee is a plastic disc, usually 20–25 cm in diameter. Players throw and catch the Frisbee, which spins through the air. Frisbees are a popular outdoor game and can commonly be seen on beaches in the summer.

The Frisbee craze hit the United States in the 1950s. Some stories suggest that the origin of the Frisbee lies with the Frisbie Baking Company in Bridgeport, Connecticut, USA, where pie pans had reportedly been thrown around by employees during their breaks, since the late 1930s.

Fred Morrison and his friend, Warren Franscioni, perfected the Frisbee in 1948 and created their company, which patented it and began Frisbee production. Prototypes were made of metal but the version developed for the public was made of plastic. As this was happening around the time of the famous Roswell incident and the UFO hysteria which subsequently followed, they called the new toy a 'Flyin-Saucer' and it was an instant and long-lasting hit.

Just Crazy!

Some fads just defy explanation! One such fad from the early twentieth century was flagpole sitting.

Flagpole Sitting

Flagpole sitting certainly comes under the heading of 'more unusual fads'. Alvin 'Shipwreck' Kelly worked as a professional stuntman in Hollywood, California, and in 1924, as a result of a dare from a friend, he attempted to sit on a flagpole. He stayed sitting on the pole for 13 hours and 13 minutes, and thereby gained the interest of the world.

Within weeks, hundreds of people were flagpole sitting. One man set a record by sitting for 12 days, then another broke the record by sitting for 21 days. The public were fascinated and huge crowds would gather to watch the latest person to have a go. In 1929, Kelly decided to reclaim the record for flagpole sitting, and in Atlantic City, New Jersey, Kelly sat on a flagpole for 49 days in front of an audience of 20,000.

By late 1929, the craze had all but died out.

Put the Spinners Down, SLIME is Here!

The next 'big thing' has arrived... and this one might stick!

Put aside the loom bands and fidget spinners: a new trend is taking over, and it probably isn't what you'd expect. SLIME has arrived, hitting schools across the globe, a sticky, gooey alternative to the play-dough we all knew as children.

Made from simple ingredients such as water, glue and food colouring, slime has quickly become so popular that many shops are beginning to sell out of the necessary ingredients.

Chloe Smith, an 11-year-old and newly-converted homemade slime addict, said, "Slime is brill! It's gooey, sticky and lots of fun to play with." Chloe has personalised her favourite slime recipe, using food colouring and even

Pupils Chloe Smith and Matilda Hilson show off the latest global craze of slime-making

little sequins for extra sparkle. She admits to spending a great deal of time and energy experimenting with ingredients to perfect her recipes but also acknowledges the mess she creates when she is concocting.

"It's fun to make but you can sometimes get it too sticky, too stretchy or too crumbly," she explained.

It would appear that there is a wealth of science behind the texture and consistency, but that in itself is not the major draw of this emerging phenomenon.

Slime can be personalised with glitter and food colouring

Matilda Hilson, a high school pupil, has been in the commercial slime business for a few months. She astutely spotted a gap in the market and now sells her slime at school, letting other pupils 'try before they buy'. This apparent altruism is, in fact, purely a marketing ploy designed to maximise sales of her product.

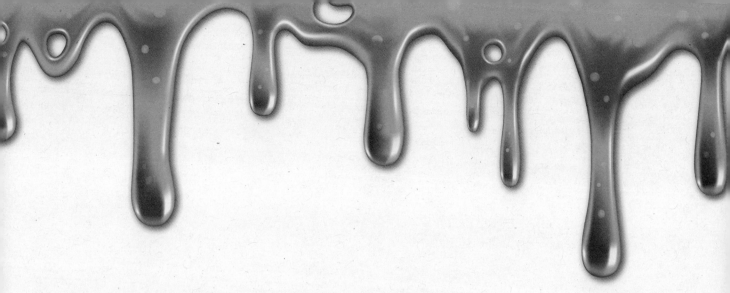

Amanda Hilson, Matilda's mum, at first loved the trend.

"I was enthusiastic because I was so pleased to see Matilda doing something creative instead of messing around with her phone."

"But it soon started to take over the place," she said. "I spend time every day cleaning the table and floors because everything has bits of slime on it."

It seems parents aren't the only ones opposed to slime.

Whilst Chloe said she uses slime to help her concentration levels in class, some teachers have banned it from the classroom. The logistics of managing a class who are manipulating a blob of slimy matter has proved a step too far.

"Our priority is teaching the children. Slime distracts them from the lesson," said Jason Cole, a head teacher. "The pupils need to stay focused."

Chloe argues that it actually helps her to focus. "The teachers think it's a distraction, but it lets me focus and stops me getting stressed."

There have been concerns about the safety of homemade slime, because of the use of borax, also known as sodium borate, which some children are adding to recipes. There have been reports of this ingredient causing burns to the skin. Lisa Hepplestone, a Leicester-based scientist, said the danger is over-exaggerated. "I actually let my own kids make slime and play with it," she said, "but I'd definitely advise against using borax. It's also important to keep it away from young children, as it should not be put near the mouth."

Enjoying the wave-crest of yet another obsessive kid-craze, ready-made slime manufacturers will soon be scrambling to be the most prominent brand on toy shop shelves.

This is a blank page

The Legend of Finn MacCool and the Giant's Causeway

A Ghost in Glasgow

The *Titanic*

Reading Booklet

Key Stage 2 English Reading Booklet – Set B

Contents

The Legend of Finn MacCool

This is the legend of the great, 16-metre tall Irish giant, Finn MacCool, who lived with his wife, Oonagh, on the hills in County Antrim in the ancient province of Ulster in Northern Ireland.

Ulster is scenically beautiful with meandering rivers, imposing cliffs and scooped-out lakes. The area is home to many mysterious stone tombs, made of vast boulders. For centuries, the Irish have known these tombs as the 'Giants' Graves' due to the legends and stories of giants.

As legend has it, one day, a Scottish giant called Benandonner started shouting across the sea at Finn MacCool, insulting him and challenging him to a fight. Finn built a causeway from Ulster across the sea to Scotland, before urging Benandonner to travel across the causeway to fight him.

But as he saw the furious Scot coming nearer, he realised Benandonner was a great deal bigger than he had previously thought so he quickly scrambled home, where he told his wife he'd stupidly challenged Benandonner to a fight but realised he probably shouldn't have.

Finn could hear Benandonner's thunderous footsteps. When Benandonner knocked on Finn's door, Finn began to shake, so quick-thinking Oonagh wrapped him in sheets to look like a baby. She'd had an idea to trick the Scottish giant and save her husband.

and the Giant's Causeway

Oonagh then opened the door to Benandonner and told him Finn was out but that he should come inside and wait for him.

Oonagh showed Benandonner around their home, pointing out Finn's spear (a huge tree) and his shield (an enormous block of wood). Benandonner thought how big and strong Finn must be if these were his weapons.

Oonagh decided she would serve Benandonner some food. She quickly cooked a cake, and put stones inside it. When Benandonner bit it, he broke some of his teeth. She then gave him a drink, which made him woolly-headed and a little unsteady on his feet. Benandonner thought how tough Finn must be if this was what he ate and drank.

Then Oonagh said to Benandonner, "Would you like to meet the baby?" and pointed to the huge 'baby'. When Benandonner saw the size of the 'baby', he thought how big Finn MacCool must be if his baby was so huge.

He dashed outside to get some fresh air and clear his head.

Oonagh showed Benandonner the gardens.
"Finn plays catch with these rocks," she said, pointing at some enormous boulders. Benandonner tried to lift a boulder, but it was so hefty he dropped it. He hurt himself a little but luckily he was a tough giant. However, he had realised that he might be out of his depth, so he made to leave hastily.

As soon as Benandonner had left, Finn grabbed a huge chunk of earth out of the ground to hurl at the retreating Scotsman. The hole in the ground became Lough Neagh. The chunk of earth he threw landed in the middle of the sea, becoming the Isle of Man.

As he fled, Benandonner ripped up the causeway, ensuring that Finn MacCool could not chase him back to Scotland.

A Ghost in Glasgow

It was mid-July, 1991, and we were in the midst of a long, warm Scottish summer. It was a balmy evening in our hometown of Glasgow. I was a young boy of 10 and my brother had just turned 13 and we lived with our parents in a rough street, in a poor part of town. From the upstairs back windows of our little terraced house we could see the cramped streets, with railway lines and the St Rollox Chemical Works beyond.

It had been another warm, sunny day and from our bedroom we could hear the shouts of other kids outside playing, laughing and mocking each other. Our old metal beds lined the far wall of the room, sitting on shabby carpet, and the cheap blankets and old furniture did nothing to brighten up the room. The ancient chest of drawers with the old-fashioned engravings and darkened metal handles had been handed down through the family for decades until it landed with us. I never liked it; there was something sinister about the dark wood and mothball smell.

At that moment, everything was so normal. Yet, just a moment later, my brother and I saw something that lives with us to this day and defies any explanation.

It was the school holidays and my brother and I had been out playing all day until we'd managed to get into a fight with a boy from the next street. When Dad got home from his job at the railway works, he'd told us off, shouted that we were little animals and sent us up to bed early with a clip around the ear. It was too early – and too light – to try to go to sleep. My brother and I sat side by side on the floor, talking, laughing and messing about, comparing cuts and bruises from our earlier fight. We talked about anything and everything, but made sure we kept our voices to a whisper. (If Dad heard us, we'd be in line for more punishment.)

It happened suddenly. One of the drawers of the old chest shot open with considerable force. A strange, grey, ghostly light drifted out, getting paler as it crossed the room. It drifted right past our faces, leaving a faint, musty smell and a barely noticeable breeze, then seemed to hover in the middle of the room. I think we were in shock. Neither of us said a word, but just sat as still as statues. Then my brother and I looked at each other in pure fear and shuffled quickly under the bed.

"What was that?" I whispered nervously when I was sure it had vanished. I hoped my brother would be able to explain it, to have a logical reason for the appearance of it, to laugh at me for being pathetic. But he could not and did not. We were rigid with shock. Of course, we'd told each other ghost stories before, each trying to frighten the other, but we'd never actually seen one.

We watched as dusk settled and listened as the sounds of kids playing out gradually faded. Eventually we fell asleep, huddled together under the bed.

When we awoke next morning, to the early chirps of the birds and the promise of another glorious summer's day, it was as if nothing had happened. We bravely checked behind the curtains and in the chest of drawers, without finding a hint or trace of what had happened. Had it not been for each of us reassuring the other that we must have imagined something – a shadow perhaps, or the bedclothes falling off the bed – I don't think I would ever have been able to sleep in that bedroom again.

The *Titanic*

Shipping in the early 20th Century

The luxury steamship RMS *Titanic* was conceived as a result of intense competition between the shipping lines in the early 20th century. Cunard and the White Star Line were striving to outdo each other and earn the title of premier shipping line. In March 1909, two years after Cunard's *Mauretania* ship began service, work began on the *Titanic* at a shipyard in Belfast.

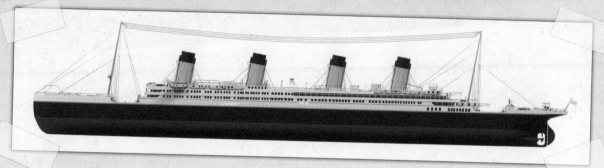

Titanic's Fate

The *Titanic* sank during her maiden voyage in the early hours of April 15, 1912. She was just off the coast of Newfoundland in the North Atlantic when she hit an iceberg. Of the 2,223 passengers and crew on board, more than 1,500 – over half – lost their lives.

The Building of the *Titanic*

Almost a year before, on May 31, 1911, *Titanic's* gigantic hull (the largest movable man-made object in the world at the time) had slowly been moved down the slipways and into Belfast's River Lagan. More than 100,000 people attended the launching. Some said that the hull was too big, and feared the worst for the ship. The hull was towed to a huge fitting out dock, where thousands of workers spent the next year building her decks and completing their fittings to the highest possible standard.

Passengers

Passengers included high-ranking officials, rich manufacturers, lords, ladies and other celebrities, including the White Star Line's managing director, J. Bruce Ismay and Thomas Andrews, the ship's chief designer.

In second class were servants of these first class passengers, plus academics and wealthy tourists. Second class on the *Titanic* was comparable to first class on other ships.

Third class held more than 700 passengers, the biggest group of passengers, some of whom had paid less than $20 to make the voyage. Third class was the main source of profit and *Titanic* offered third class passengers accommodation and facilities grander than those in third class on any other ship.

The Sinking of the *Titanic*

On April 10, 1912, the ill-fated vessel set off. The initial stages of her voyage were not completely without hindrance: a small coal fire in a bunker had to be put out. Furthermore, as she pulled out of Southampton dock, she narrowly missed a collision with another ship. Some superstitious *Titanic* experts claim this is the worst kind of omen for a ship's maiden voyage.

The journey was uneventful for four days. There were some occasional warnings of ice from other ships, but the sea was calm and she was sailing well so there seemed to be no reason for alarm.

At about 11:30 p.m., a lookout noticed an iceberg directly ahead, so rang the warning bell and telephoned the bridge. The engines were reversed and the ship was turned hard. The *Titanic* scraped along the side of the iceberg, scattering ice on the deck.

At first, it was assumed that a collision had been avoided. However, the iceberg had gouged a 300-foot hole in the hull below the waterline.

The captain toured the damaged area but five compartments had already begun filling with water, and the bow of the fated ship was sloped downward, allowing seawater to pour from one bulkhead into the next. Calculating that the *Titanic* might remain afloat for perhaps an hour and a half, he called for help and ordered the lifeboats to be filled and lowered.

The evacuation was disorganised. When the first lifeboat was lowered to the sea, instead of holding 65 people, it held only 28. Nearly every lifeboat was launched in this way, some with only a handful of passengers. There were just 16 boats in total, plus four collapsible boats, which could only accommodate a total of 1,178 people. The *Titanic* was carrying her full capacity of 2,223 passengers and crew. While hugely inadequate by today's standards, *Titanic* actually had more lifeboats than were required by law.

Women and children boarded the boats first; only when there were no women or children nearby were men permitted aboard. But many of the victims were in fact women and children, due to disorganised procedures that did not manage to get them to the boats.

First class passenger Molly Brown had been helping people into lifeboats when she was made to get into the last one. She implored its crewmen to turn back for survivors, but they refused, for fear the boat would be overturned by desperate survivors struggling in the sea.

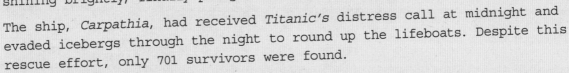

Thomas Andrews was witnessed in the first class smoking room, staring vacantly at a painting. The wealthiest passenger on board, John Jacob Astor IV placed his wife into a lifeboat and, pronouncing that she was pregnant, asked to go with her; his request was refused.

At 2:20 a.m. on April 15th, almost three hours after hitting the iceberg, *Titanic*, almost completely vertical and with many of her lights still shining brightly, finally plunged beneath the ocean.

The ship, *Carpathia*, had received *Titanic's* distress call at midnight and evaded icebergs through the night to round up the lifeboats. Despite this rescue effort, only 701 survivors were found.

Titanic's Legacy

Whilst the sinking of the *Titanic* was a terrible tragedy, it is also linked with stories of selflessness, love and heroism. Despite the many technical and safety questions raised, *Titanic's* demise is an example of the power of nature and mankind's over-reliance on technology. The ship's makers believed they had constructed an unsinkable ship that could not be conquered by nature, but the tragedy highlighted that humans cannot defeat nature.

This is a blank page

Key Stage 2

English reading

Set A: Reading answer booklet

Name						
School						
Date of Birth	Day		Month		Year	

Instructions

Questions and answers

You have **one hour** to complete this test. Read one text and answer all the questions about that text before moving on to the next text. There are three texts and three sets of test questions.

There are different types of question, which you need to answer in different ways.

Short answers
Some questions have a short answer line or answer box. You only need to write a word or a few words for your answer.

Several line answers
Some questions have a few answer lines. You need to write more words or a sentence or two for your answer.

Longer answers
Some questions have more answer lines. You need to write a longer, more detailed answer to give your opinion. You may write in full sentences.

Selected answers
Some questions require you to tick, draw lines to, or circle the correct answer.

The space provided shows you what type of answer is required. You must write your answer in the space provided.

Always read the instructions carefully so you know how to answer the question.

Marks

The numbers at the side of the page tell you the number of marks for each question.

This is a reading test, so you need to use the information in the texts to answer the questions.

When a question includes a paragraph or page reference, you should refer to that paragraph or page to help you with your answer.

1 Look at the first paragraph, beginning: _Peter whined and complained..._

What is the weather like on the walk home?

Tick **one**.

It is a hot sunny day. ☐

It is cold and icy. ☐

It is raining. ☐

There is a cool breeze. ☐

1 mark

2 _Peter thought George was a_ **spoilt** _show-off._

Which word is closest in meaning to _spoilt_?

Tick **one**.

indulged ☐

tempted ☐

disgraceful ☐

damaged ☐

1 mark

3 Why does Peter feel he is treated badly?

_____

_____ 1 mark

4 When they arrive home, Peter sulks in his room.

What could be his motivation for doing this?

_____ 1 mark

5 What two obsessions does Mum remember Peter having in the past?

_____

_____ 1 mark

6 *After a very subdued meal...*

What does 'a very subdued meal' mean?

_____

_____ 1 mark

7 *...strewn across his bedroom floor.*

What does the word 'strewn' tell you about the toys in Peter's room?

_____

_____
1 mark

8 How does Peter feel when Mohammed comes over to him?

_____

_____
1 mark

9 How do you think Peter's mother feels about his behaviour?

Use two examples from the text to justify your answer.

_____

_____

_____

_____
2 marks

10 *He considered the situation his new friend was in…*

What does 'considered the situation his new friend was in' mean in this sentence?

Peter was thinking about Mohammed being in his room. ☐

Peter was thinking about what toys Mohammed could give him. ☐

Peter was seeing someone else's point of view for once. ☐

Peter felt angry with Mohammed. ☐

1 mark

11 What do you think Peter will say to Mum next time he sees her?

Give a reason for your answer.

_____

_____

2 marks

12 Peter recognises that Mohammed has had a difficult and frightening time.

Who told Peter about Mohammed's situation?

_____

1 mark

13 The final sentence states, 'Suddenly, Peter realised something …'.

What do you think Peter might have realised and what do you think he might change?

_____

_____

_____

_____

14 *When popular celebrities of the day such as Elvis Presley began to wear this style of trouser, the trend was quickly taken up by young people, who viewed them as a fashionable contrast to the straight-legged and more conservative trousers worn by the older generation.*

Find and **copy two** words from the passage above which show that bellbottoms were well-liked:

1. _____

2. _____

1 mark

15 Which major event in history ultimately led to the development of the modern leisure suit?

_____

1 mark

16 Look at the paragraph beginning: *From a simple hoop or ball…*

Find and **copy one** word or group of words from this paragraph that is closest in meaning to 'advanced'.

_____

1 mark

17 Using information from the text, put a tick in the correct box to show whether each statement is **true** or **false**.

	True	False
Bellbottomed trousers were originally designed for the army.		
Frisbees are usually 20–25 cm in diameter.		
Cabbage Patch Kids were invented in the 1890s.		
The Frisbee craze hit the United States in the 1950s.		

1 mark

18 Name two crazes and give **one** downside for each craze. Describe how these were dealt with.

1. Downside: _____

   How it was dealt with: _____

2. Downside: _____

   How it was dealt with: _____

2 marks

19 What two things did each Cabbage Patch Kid come with?

_____

_____
2 marks

20 Look at the paragraph beginning: *Originally the invention of 21-year-old Xavier Roberts…*

Find and **copy** the words which tell us that sales of Cabbage Patch Kids across the world grew enormously.

1 mark

_____

21 Look at the section about **Frisbees**.

In what year did Franscioni and Morrison perfect the Frisbee?

1 mark

_____

22 According to some stories, from which country did Frisbees originate?

_____
1 mark

23 Frisbees became popular at a time when many people were fascinated with UFOs.

Give **one** word from the text which highlights how people felt about UFOs.

_____
1 mark

24 Look at the section about **flagpole sitting**.

What was Kelly's record for staying on the pole?

_____
1 mark

25 Put a tick in the correct box to show whether each of the following statements is a **fact** or an **opinion**.

	Fact	Opinion
Kelly's first attempt lasted 13 hours and 13 minutes.		
Alvin Kelly only did reckless things in his lifetime.		
20,000 people watched Kelly in Atlantic City.		
Flagpole sitting was the most unusual fad of the 20th century.		

1 mark

26 Which of the following would be the most suitable summary of the whole text?

Tick **one**.

A brief history of crazes and fads through the decades. ☐

The life stories of those who invented the crazes. ☐

A list of crazes you should try. ☐

A story about someone who tried some crazes out. ☐

1 mark

27 Draw lines to match each section to its main content.

One has been done for you.

Toys	A description of one of the more unusual crazes from the past
Fashion	Details about some popular and successful playthings
Just Crazy!	An overview and introduction
Fads, Crazes and Trends over Time	The history and beginnings of fashions in clothing

Toys — Details about some popular and successful playthings

1 mark

28 Look at the paragraph beginning: *Chloe Smith, an 11-year-old and newly-converted homemade slime addict...*

What potential academic benefit could there be to this craze?

_____

_____

1 mark

29 What makes the slime so appealing?

Give **two** reasons, using evidence from the text to support your answer.

_____

_____

_____

_____

_____

_____

_____

3 marks

30 a) *"… you can sometimes get it too sticky, too stretchy or too crumbly,"*
she explained.

What does this sentence tell us about Chloe's experiences of making slime?

_____

_____

1 mark

b) *She admits to spending a great deal of time and energy experimenting*
with ingredients to perfect her recipes but also acknowledges the mess
she creates when she is concocting.

How might Chloe's slime-making cause problems?

_____

_____

1 mark

31 Look at the paragraph beginning: *Matilda Hilson, a high school pupil…*

What does this tell us about Matilda's character?

Explain **two** features of her character, using evidence from the text to support
your answer.

_____

_____

_____

_____

_____

_____

3 marks

32 **Find** and **copy two** words or groups of words which show that Matilda Hilson is a good businesswoman.

1. _____

2. _____

33 *"But it soon started to take over the place,"*

How did Amanda's attitude to slime change?

Tick **one**.

At first she hated it, but then she played with some and loved it. ☐

At first, she was frightened of it but then she made herself try it. ☐

At first she loved the idea, but then it became an issue. ☐

At first she liked it, but now she loves it. ☐

34 Which two things does Amanda Hilson say she must clean frequently and why?

_____

_____

_____

35 *...yet another obsessive kid-craze.*

What does this description suggest about the craze?

_____

_____

1 mark

36 *Lisa Hepplestone, a Leicester-based scientist, said the danger is over-exaggerated.*

This tells us that slime is probably...

Tick **one**.

overrated.   ☐

unexciting.   ☐

safe to use.   ☐

potentially explosive.   ☐

1 mark

37 *Enjoying the wave-crest of yet another obsessive kid-craze, ready-made slime manufacturers will soon be scrambling to be the most prominent brand on toy shop shelves.*

Choose the best words to match the description above. Circle both of your choices.

Ready-made slime

buyers	makers	sellers	users

_____
1 mark

are scrambling to be the

cheapest	most expensive	most visible	most disgusting

_____
1 mark

38 Tick one box in each row to show whether each statement is **true** or **false**.

	True	False
Slime can be made from glue.		
Borax is also known as sodium borate.		
Adults are all opposed to slime.		
Slime can be personalised.		

1 mark

Key Stage 2

English grammar, punctuation and spelling

Set A
Paper 1: questions

Name						
School						
Date of Birth	Day		Month		Year	

Instructions

1 | Draw a line to match each word to the correct **suffix** to make an adjective.

Word
fear
read
slow

Suffix
able
ly
less

1 mark

2 | Draw a line to match each sentence to the correct **determiner**. Use each determiner only once.

Sentence
At the supermarket, I bought _____ peaches.
I also bought _____ avocado.
I carried all _____ shopping home.

Determiner
the
some
an

1 mark

3 | Circle the **object** in the sentence below.

My mother brought a snack for me after school.

1 mark

4 | Complete the sentence below by writing the **conjunctions** from the box in the correct places. Use each conjunction only once.

if	and	but

We should bring coats _____ umbrellas _____ the weather

looks poor, _____ we should also bring sun cream just in case!

1 mark

5 | Tick the option that must end with a **question mark**.

Tick **one**.

I will play with Jake at break time ☐

Shall I play with Jake today ☐

Jake and I played together ☐

I asked Jake to play with me ☐

1 mark

6 | Complete the sentence with an appropriate **adverb**.

He slammed the car door _____.

1 mark

7 | Which sentence uses the **colon** correctly?

Tick **one**.

I needed several ingredients some flour:
two eggs, sugar and a vanilla pod. ☐

I needed: several ingredients some flour,
two eggs, sugar and a vanilla pod. ☐

I needed several: ingredients some flour,
two eggs, sugar and a vanilla pod. ☐

I needed several ingredients: some flour,
two eggs, sugar and a vanilla pod. ☐

1 mark

8 Tick four boxes to show where the missing **inverted commas** should go.

☐   ☐   ☐   ☐

When we have finished our writing, said the teacher, we will start a new topic.

☐   ☐

1 mark

9 Insert one **comma** in the correct place in the sentence below.

Glancing   behind   her   the   girl   continued   down   the   street.

1 mark

10 Replace the underlined word or words in each sentence with the correct **pronoun**.

When the children had finished playing, <u>the children</u> _____ tidied away all the toys.

Dad was so impressed with the tidy room, <u>Dad</u> _____ gave all the children a treat.

1 mark

11 Tick one box in each row to show if the sentence is in the **present progressive** or the **past progressive tense**.

Sentence	Present progressive	Past progressive
Sara is getting excited about the birthday party.		
Sara was talking about which present to choose.		
Sara is preparing a surprise for her friend.		

1 mark

12 Which sentence uses the **hyphen** correctly?

Tick **one**.

The kind-hearted girl raised money for charity. ☐

The kind-hearted-girl raised money for charity. ☐

The kind-hearted girl raised money for-charity. ☐

The kind hearted-girl raised money for charity. ☐

1 mark

13 Which sentence shows that you are **least likely** to be able to help?

Tick **one**.

I won't be available to help. ☐

I might be available to help. ☐

I could be available to help. ☐

I will be available to help. ☐

1 mark

14 Draw a line to match each sentence to its correct **function**. Use each function only once.

Sentence	Function
What a coincidence it was	question
Did you enjoy the trip to the theatre	command
There were 20 people at the park	exclamation
Put the bags down and come inside	statement

1 mark

15 Which sentence is written in **Standard English**?

Tick **one**.

I went to my friends and done some games. ☐

I travelled to France to visit my sister. ☐

He seen them as they came up the road. ☐

They was going on their bikes. ☐

1 mark

16 Replace the underlined words in the sentences below with their **expanded** forms.

She'll _____ call round when

we've _____ eaten dinner.

I don't _____ know why.

1 mark

17 a) What is the name of the punctuation marks on either side of the words who was his best friend in the sentence below?

James met Joe (who was his best friend) in the park after school.

_____

1 mark

b) What is the name of a different punctuation mark that could be used correctly in the same place?

_____

1 mark

18 You are helping a friend to correct the punctuation in the sentence below.

Which two pieces of advice should you give to correct the **punctuation**?

"Can you lend me a pencil" asked the boy!

Tick **two**.

The sentence should end with a full stop instead of an exclamation mark. ☐

There should be a question mark after the inverted commas. ☐

There should be a comma after the word can. ☐

There should be an exclamation mark after the word asked. ☐

There should be a question mark after the word pencil. ☐

1 mark

19 Which sentence uses **capital letters** correctly?

Tick **one**.

In april, my Cousin will fly from london to Rome for a Holiday. ☐

In April, my cousin will fly from London to Rome for a holiday. ☐

In April, my cousin will Fly from London to rome for a holiday. ☐

In april, my cousin will fly from London To Rome for a holiday. ☐

1 mark

20 Insert a **semi-colon** in the correct place in the sentence below.

My friends are going shopping they need new uniform for school.

1 mark

21 Circle the word in the sentence that contains an **apostrophe** for possession.

I can't seem to find Claire's phone number and I'm supposed to call her later on.

1 mark

22 What does the root <u>min</u> mean in the **word family** below?

minority, **min**uscule, **min**ute

Tick **one**.

plenty ☐

small ☐

on the outside ☐

loud or noisy ☐

1 mark

23 Tick one box in each row to show whether the **commas** are used correctly or incorrectly in the sentence.

Sentence	Commas used correctly	Commas used incorrectly
We should buy some cheese, bread and a box of eggs.		
They ran all, over the field looking for their lost dog.		
My wallet, old and worn, is never very full of money.		
She looked at the clock and, realised she was late.		

1 mark

24 Circle all the **prepositions** in the sentence below.

They ran under the bridge and hid behind a large bush.

1 mark

25 Rearrange the words in the statement below to make it a **question**.
Use only the given words.
Remember to punctuate your sentence correctly.

He was talking to the police.

_____

1 mark

26 Circle the two words that show the **tense** in the sentence below.

He bit into his sandwich just as the train came into the station.

1 mark

27 Explain the purpose of the **subordinate clause** in the sentence below.

Sam would not go into the water because it was so cold.

_____

_____

1 mark

28 Circle the **conjunction** in each sentence below.

Put the kitten down before you drop her.

I hung out all the washing, although the rain clouds were darkening.

1 mark

29 Tick one box in each row to show whether the underlined clause is a **main clause** or a **subordinate clause**.

	Main clause	Subordinate clause
The light was fading <u>because it was nearly evening time.</u>		
The kettle, <u>which was brand new,</u> began to boil.		
When the clock struck twelve, <u>my tummy began to rumble.</u>		

1 mark

30 a) Insert a **comma** in the sentence below to make it clear that only Joe and Kate went bowling.

Once they had asked Mum Joe and Kate went bowling.

1 mark

b) Insert commas in the sentence below to make it clear that all three went bowling.

Once they had asked Mum Joe and Kate went bowling.

1 mark

31 Circle the two **conjunctions** in the sentence below.

The puppy wagged his tail furiously, but Jack took no notice and went inside the house.

1 mark

32 Explain how the different **prefixes** change the meanings of the two sentences below.

The customer complained that the chicken was uncooked.

This means that the chicken _____

The customer complained that the chicken was overcooked.

This means that the chicken _____

1 mark

33 Replace the underlined word or words in each sentence with the correct **possessive pronoun**.

That doll belongs to <u>my sister</u>. The doll is _____.

The car belongs to <u>them</u>. The car is _____.

The keys belong to <u>us</u>. The keys are _____.

1 mark

34 a) Write an explanation of the word **synonym**.

_____

_____

1 mark

b) Write one word that is a **synonym** of <u>frightened</u>.

_____

1 mark

35 Complete the sentences below, using the **simple past tense** of the verbs in the boxes.

Last Tuesday, the family (go) _____ out for a walk. They (walk)

_____ through some woods and (see) _____

lots of wildlife.

1 mark

36 Complete the passage with **adjectives** derived from the nouns in brackets. One has been done for you.

Even though she felt (nerve) _____ nervous _____, Chloe reached

out to touch the unicorn's (beauty) _____ mane.

It was a (magic) _____ experience.

1 mark

37 Which option correctly completes the sentence below?

The person _____ responsible will be caught and punished.

Tick **one**.

whose ☐

who's ☐

which ☐

whom ☐

1 mark

38 Write a sentence using the word <u>wish</u> as a **verb**.
Do not change the word.
Remember to punctuate your sentence correctly.

_____

_____

1 mark

Write a sentence using the word <u>wish</u> as a **noun**.
Do not change the word.
Remember to punctuate your sentence correctly.

_____

_____

1 mark

39 Underline the **relative clause** in the sentence below.

The new car which is parked on our driveway is in need of a wash.

1 mark

40 Tick one box in each row to show whether the sentence is written in the **active voice** or the **passive voice**.

Sentence	Active	Passive
The chocolate bar was melted by the sun.		
The children washed the windows.		
The candles were blown out by the boy.		

1 mark

41 Circle the two **adverbs** in the sentence below.

The children were playing noisily, so I had to step outside.

1 mark

42 Rewrite the sentence below so that it is in the **active voice**. Remember to punctuate your sentence correctly.

The prisoner was sentenced by the judge.

_____

_____

1 mark

43 Tick the option which shows how the underlined words in the sentence below are used.

The rich chocolate fudge cake was a huge success.

Tick one.

as a main clause ☐

as a fronted adverbial ☐

as a subordinate clause ☐

as an expanded noun phrase ☐

1 mark

44 Complete the sentence with the verb 'to be' in its **subjunctive form**.

If I _____ you, I would say yes.

1 mark

45 Explain how you know this sentence is in the **present perfect form**.

My sister has finished all of her homework.

_____

_____

1 mark

46 What punctuation would be most appropriate to replace the full stop at the end of this sentence?

How proud you've made me. ☐

1 mark

English grammar, punctuation and spelling

Set A
Paper 2: spelling

Questions and answers

You have approximately **15 minutes** to complete this test.

You will need someone to read the instructions and sentences to you. These can be found in the Contents, Instructions and Answers booklet.

Marks

Each spelling question is worth 1 mark.

Name	
School	

Date of Birth	Day		Month		Year	

Spelling task

1 There has been some kind of _____.

2 I have _____ my best friend for many years.

3 He secretly _____ the conversation.

4 Sam is the most _____ person I know.

5 He _____ fruit to vegetables.

6 I came to a startling _____.

7 I fear the house has been _____.

8 There is a huge _____ in clothes sizes.

9 We must remember to buy _____ for the holiday.

10 Even _____ I was afraid, I stood up to speak.

11 The ships were docked at the _____.

12 The _____ king was not popular among his subjects.

13 Most children have _____ education at school.

14 The _____ captivated the young children.

15 The _____ rain lasted for several hours.

16 Astronauts experience _____ in space.

17 I keep _____ where I've put my keys.

18 Keep the _____ in case you need to return it.

19 I won a prize in the _____.

20 The dog _____ attacked the new toy.

This is a blank page

Key Stage 2

English reading

Set B: Reading answer booklet

Name						
School						
Date of Birth	Day		Month		Year	

Instructions

Questions and answers

You have **one hour** to complete this test. Read one text and answer all the questions about that text before moving on to the next text. There are three texts and three sets of test questions.

There are different types of question, which you need to answer in different ways.

Short answers

Some questions have a short answer line or answer box. You only need to write a word or a few words for your answer.

Several line answers

Some questions have a few answer lines. You need to write more words or a sentence or two for your answer.

Longer answers

Some questions have more answer lines. You need to write a longer, more detailed answer to give your opinion. You may write in full sentences.

Selected answers

Some questions require you to tick, draw lines to, or circle the correct answer.

The space provided shows you what type of answer is required. You must write your answer in the space provided.

Always read the instructions carefully so you know how to answer the question.

Marks

The numbers at the side of the page tell you the number of marks for each question.

This is a reading test, so you need to use the information in the texts to answer the questions.

When a question includes a paragraph or page reference, you should refer to that paragraph or page to help you with your answer.

1 Look at the paragraph beginning: *Ulster is scenically beautiful...*

Find and **copy one** word meaning 'rocks'.

_____

1 mark

2 *...imposing cliffs and scooped-out lakes.*

Which word most closely matches the meaning of the word 'imposing'?

Tick one.

impressive ☐

underwhelming ☐

forceful ☐

important ☐

1 mark

3 *... meandering rivers, imposing cliffs and scooped-out lakes.*

What does this tell you about the water?

Give **two**.

1. _____

2. _____

2 marks

4 Look at the paragraph beginning: *But as he saw the furious Scot coming nearer...*

How can you tell Finn has made a mistake?

_____

_____
1 mark

5 Identify **two** things from the text that indicate that Finn realised he had made a big mistake in urging Benandonner to fight him.

_____

_____

_____
1 mark

6 Look at the paragraph beginning:

Oonagh then opened the door to Benandonner...

to the paragraph ending:

... He dashed outside to get some fresh air and clear his head.

What does this tell you about Finn's wife?

Give **two**.

1. _____

2. _____
1 mark

7 Write down three things Finn's wife does to fool the Scottish giant.

1. _____

2. _____

3. _____ 3 marks

8 Which of the following words could be used to describe Finn?

Tick one.

Inconsolable ☐

Underpaid ☐

Overconfident ☐

Uninvolved ☐ 1 mark

9 Look at the paragraph beginning: *Oonagh showed Benandonner the gardens.*

a) What did Benandonner struggle to do?

_____ 1 mark

b) Why was Benandonner fortunate?

_____ 1 mark

10 What body of land was allegedly formed at the end of the story?

Tick **one**.

The Giant's Causeway ☐

The Kingdom of Ulster ☐

The Isle of Man ☐

Robertstown ☐

1 mark

11 Using information from the text, tick one box in each row to show whether each statement is **true** or **false**.

	True	False
Finn felt great affection for the Scottish giant.		
Finn built the causeway to make friends with the Scottish giant.		
Finn was married.		
Finn underestimated the size of the Scottish giant.		

2 marks

12 Circle the correct option to complete each sentence below.

a) The story is set in…

summer.	autumn.

winter.	spring.

1 mark

b) The boys had been….

playing at home.	practising their guitars.

playing with another boy.	fighting with another boy.

1 mark

c) Their father…

fed them their dinner, made them wash up and sent them outside.	read them a story, gave them milk and gave them a bath.

told them off, gave them a clip around the ear and sent them to bed.	made them a drink, gave them a biscuit and told them to go to bed.

1 mark

d) The next morning they…

loudly told their story.	nervously checked the bed.

bravely checked the chest of drawers.	quietly said a prayer.

1 mark

13 Read the paragraph beginning: *It was the school holidays...*

How do you know it is not the boys' usual bedtime?

_____

1 mark

14 *If Dad heard us, we'd be in line for more punishment.*

Explain what this suggests about what the boys know of Dad's personality or character.

_____

_____

2 marks

15 What evidence tells us that the siblings were actually quite close?

Tick **two**.

The boys had to share a bedroom. ☐

The boys sat side by side and chatted. ☐

The boys huddled together when they saw the ghost. ☐

The boys had the same bed. ☐

The boys kept their voices down. ☐

1 mark

16 a) What evidence is there to suggest that the boys were absolutely terrified by what they saw? Give **two** points.

_____

_____ 2 marks

b) What evidence is there to show that the boys tried to dismiss what they had seen?

_____

_____ 1 mark

17 What evidence is there in the text that this is not a wealthy family?

Give **two** examples.

1. _____

2. _____ 2 marks

18 What inspired the size and scale of the *Titanic*?

_____

1 mark

19 Why did it take almost a year from the launch of the *Titanic's* hull to her maiden voyage?

_____

_____

1 mark

20 Where did the *Titanic* sink?

_____

1 mark

21 Do you think the White Star Line learned any lessons from what happened to the *Titanic*?

Tick **one**.

Yes ☐

No ☐

Explain your choice fully, using evidence from the text.

_____

_____

_____

_____

_____
3 marks

22 Why do you think so many people wanted to be on board the *Titanic* for her inaugural voyage?

Give at least two points and explain them fully, referring to the text in your answer.

_____

_____

_____

_____

_____

_____
3 marks

23 Draw lines to match each part of the recount with the correct quotation from the text.

Before the building began	Despite the many technical and safety questions raised, *Titanic*'s demise is an example of the power of nature and mankind's over-reliance on technology.
During the building process	There were some occasional warnings of ice from other ships, but the sea was calm and she was sailing well so there seemed to be no reason for alarm.
During the voyage	The hull was towed to a huge fitting out dock, where thousands of workers spent the next year building her decks and completing the fittings to the highest possible standard.
After the tragedy	Cunard and the White Star Line were striving to outdo each other.

1 mark

24 *Third class held more than 700 passengers, the biggest group of passengers.*

Why do you think this was the case?

_____

_____ 1 mark

25 According to the text, how might the servants' expectations of the ship have been exceeded?

_____ 1 mark

26 Look at the paragraph beginning: *On April 10, 1912, the ill-fated vessel set off.*

Find the word, or group of words, which tells us that the beginning of the voyage was not completely straightforward.

_____ 1 mark

27 a) Give **two** reasons why some may have considered the voyage ill-fated right from the beginning.

1. _____

2. _____ 1 mark

b) List **two** things that the captain did on finding the damage to the hull.

1. _____

2. _____ 1 mark

28 **Find** and **copy one** word from the paragraph beginning: *Women and children boarded the boats first...* which tells you that the procedures for evacuation were not very structured.

_____ 1 mark

29 Look at the paragraph beginning: *First class passenger Molly Brown...*

What does the word 'implored' tell you about the way Molly asked the crewmen to turn around?

_____

_____ 1 mark

30 What was the name of the richest passenger on board the *Titanic*?

_____ 1 mark

31 *The ship,* Carpathia, *had received* Titanic's *distress call at midnight and evaded icebergs through the night to round up the lifeboats.*

Give the meaning of the word 'evaded' in this sentence.

_____ 1 mark

32 What does 'humans cannot defeat nature' mean?

Tick **one**.

the winner in a nature competition ☐

conquering Mother Nature ☐

making the best of the weather ☐

unable to conquer the elements ☐

1 mark

33 Below are some summaries of different paragraphs from the text.

Number them 1–6 to show the order in which they appear in the text.

The first one has been done for you.

The aftermath	
Opposition and rivalry	1
Construction commences	
Alarm bells and damages	
Sinking of the ship	
Chaotic evacuation	

1 mark

Key Stage 2

English grammar, punctuation and spelling

Set B
Paper 1: questions

Name						
School						
Date of Birth	Day		Month		Year	

Instructions

Questions and answers

You have **45 minutes** to complete this test.

There are different types of question which you need to answer in different ways. The space for your answer shows you what type of answer is needed. You must write your answer in the space provided.

Multiple-choice answers

Some questions require you to tick, draw lines to, or circle the correct answer.

Short answers

Some questions have a line or a box. You only need to write a word, a few words or a sentence for your answer.

Read the instructions carefully so you know how to answer each question.

Marks

The numbers at the side of the page tell you the number of marks for each question.

You should work as quickly and as carefully as you can. If you finish before the end of the test, go back and check your answers.

1 Tick the sentence that must end with a **question mark**.

Tick **one**.

Why they would consider that is anyone's guess ☐

What she was doing there is unclear ☐

How he got stuck remains a secret ☐

At what point did you give up ☐

1 mark

2 Insert a **semi-colon** in the correct place in the sentence below.

Go and visit your grandmother she is expecting you.

1 mark

3 Explain the effect of replacing the underlined word with a pronoun.

Harry is arriving from Leeds on Tuesday. Harry is visiting his grandmother.

_____

_____

1 mark

4 The **prefix** <u>dis-</u> can be added to the word <u>lodge</u> to make the word <u>dislodge</u>.

What does the word <u>dislodge</u> mean?

Tick **one**.

To deny ☐

To force out of position ☐

To install ☐

To repair ☐

1 mark

5 Which **verb form** completes the sentence?

Whilst Fran _____ the dishes, the doorbell rang.

Tick **one**.

had washed ☐

is washing ☐

was washing ☐

has washed ☐

1 mark

6 Circle the correct **verb form** in each underlined pair to complete the sentences below.

The streamers and balloons (<u>was/were</u>) very brightly-coloured.

The first time I saw tigers and lions (<u>was/were</u>) at the zoo.

My cousins (<u>was/were</u>) excited about visiting in the holidays.

1 mark

7 Tick the option that correctly uses **commas**.

Tick **one**.

Without, hesitation Miles accepted the offer of a place at the university. ☐

Without hesitation Miles accepted, the offer of a place at the university. ☐

Without hesitation, Miles accepted the offer of a place at the university. ☐

Without hesitation Miles, accepted the offer of a place at the university. ☐

1 mark

8 Which sentence is punctuated correctly?

Tick **one**.

Noah brushed his teeth put on his pyjamas, turned out his lamp and went to sleep. ☐

Noah brushed his teeth, put on his pyjamas, turned out his lamp and went to sleep. ☐

Noah brushed his teeth, put on his pyjamas, turned out his lamp, and went to sleep. ☐

Noah brushed, his teeth put on his, pyjamas turned out his, lamp and went to sleep. ☐

1 mark

9 | What is the **word class** of the underlined word in the sentence below?

I started packing and <u>quickly</u> realised my suitcase was too small.

Tick **one**.

conjunction ☐

adverb ☐

verb ☐

determiner ☐

1 mark

10 | Tick one box to show the correct place for a **colon** in the sentence below.

☐ ☐ ☐

I have four best friends Tom (my brother), Sam, James and Nathan.

☐ ☐

1 mark

11 | What is the **word class** of the underlined words in the sentence below?

We put <u>the</u> cutlery in <u>a</u> drawer and <u>some</u> spoons on <u>the</u> shelf.

Tick **one**.

adjectives ☐

adverbs ☐

determiners ☐

nouns ☐

1 mark

12 | Which sentence is punctuated correctly?

Tick **one**.

I love going swimming – it's a great way to keep fit. ☐

I love going – swimming it's a great way – to keep fit. ☐

I love going swimming it's a great way to keep-fit. ☐

I love – going swimming it's a great way to keep fit. ☐

1 mark

13 | Which sentence uses the word <u>firm</u> as an **adjective**?

Tick **one**.

You must stand firm. ☐

Please firm up the prices of these stamps. ☐

Ben had a firm grip on the trophy. ☐

The firm was being investigated by the police. ☐

1 mark

14 | Which sentence is punctuated correctly?

Tick **one**.

The flask holds 1 litre (1000) millilitres of liquid. ☐

The flask holds (1 litre 1000 millilitres) of liquid. ☐

The flask holds 1 litre (1000 millilitres of liquid). ☐

The flask holds 1 litre (1000 millilitres) of liquid. ☐

1 mark

15 Explain the use of an **adverb** in a sentence.

_____

_____

1 mark

16 Complete the sentence with an appropriate **subordinating conjunction**.

We stopped off for a drink _____ it was a hot day.

1 mark

17 Which sentence is an **exclamation**?

Tick **one**.

How much pizza have you eaten ☐

He rather enjoyed his pizza ☐

What a lot of pizza you have eaten ☐

I said we should have pizza sometime ☐

1 mark

18 Which sentence uses the word <u>chip</u> as a **verb**?

Tick **one**.

The cup had a huge chip on one side. ☐

I asked her for a chip from her plate. ☐

My credit card uses chip and pin technology. ☐

I began to chip at the dried plaster. ☐

1 mark

19 Suggest a **preposition** to add to the sentence below.

The young child looked carefully _____ crossing the busy road.

1 mark

20 Replace the underlined word or words in the sentence below with the correct **pronouns**.

Sarah asked her parents for some pocket money but <u>her parents</u>

_____ asked <u>Sarah</u> _____ to clean out the

rabbit hutch first.

1 mark

21 Which sentence is punctuated correctly?

Tick **one**.

"The teacher asked Who owns this bag?" ☐

The teacher asked, "Who owns this bag?" ☐

The teacher asked "Who owns this bag" ☐

The teacher asked, "who owns this bag?" ☐

1 mark

22 Which sentence is the most **formal**?

Tick **one**.

We'd love to see you at the party later on. ☐

You are cordially invited to a party. ☐

We're having a party – can you come? ☐

You'd love to come to the party at our house, wouldn't you? ☐

1 mark

23 Which underlined group of words is a **subordinate clause**?

Tick **one**.

The class, <u>which is mainly boys</u>, loves science lessons. ☐

<u>The clock shows 3 o'clock</u> although it is nearly 4 o'clock. ☐

<u>Hettie</u>, who is a sweet girl, <u>has lots of friends</u>. ☐

When it's Christmas, <u>the family gets together</u>. ☐

1 mark

24 Circle the two words that are **antonyms** in the sentence below.

Despite the twins appearing to be identical, they are actually different in many ways.

1 mark

25 Tick one box in each row to show whether the **apostrophe** is used for omission or possession.

	Apostrophe for omission	Apostrophe for possession
My mother's friend is called Tina.		
We're going away tomorrow.		
The dog's collar is broken.		
She's bringing some cakes tomorrow.		

1 mark

26 Which sentence contains a **relative clause**?

Tick **one**.

The kite is flying above the beach. ☐

A girl who I know from school is coming to karate class. ☐

Andy knows where the dog food is kept. ☐

Because of the late hour, I sent everyone to bed. ☐

1 mark

27 Which sentence is a **statement**?

Tick **one**.

Are you looking forward to the trip ☐

Please put on your shoes and coat ☐

What a disaster ☐

I will pack a picnic for everyone to share ☐

1 mark

28 Insert **full stops** and **capital letters** in the passage below so it is punctuated correctly.

Jane picked up the full rubbish bag she carried it to the bin

she opened the lid but an enormous split appeared in the bag

there was rubbish all over the floor

1 mark

29 Insert a **pair of commas** in the correct place in the sentence below.

The team which was made up of children at my school won

the match easily.

1 mark

30 Rewrite the **verbs** in the brackets to complete the sentences with the correct choice of tense.

The mice (to nibble) _____ at the corner of the box of cat food.

Josh (to speak) _____ very softly when he gave his

reasons for leaving.

1 mark

31 Write a **command** which could be the first step in the instructions for brushing your teeth.

Remember to punctuate your answer correctly.

_____

_____

1 mark

32 Label each of the clauses in the sentence below as either **main (M)** or **subordinate (S)**.

☐   ☐

As the book was so interesting, I found myself reading it often and

offered to share it with the class.

☐

1 mark

33 Circle the **conjunction** in each sentence.

They bought new running shoes when the sale was on.

Although the weather was poor, they were determined to cross the finish line.

The race went extremely well, so they decided to sign up for another.

1 mark

34 Which two sentences contain a **preposition**?

Tick **two**.

The tortoise moved very slowly towards the lettuce. ☐

The clown juggled and made the children laugh. ☐

My cat walked carefully along the garden fence. ☐

I am planning to make a necklace this year. ☐

1 mark

35 Underline the **subject** of the sentence below.

Before leaving the house, John remembered to pick up his wallet.

1 mark

36 Write a sentence containing a **conjunction** expressing cause.

_____

_____

1 mark

37 Circle the **relative pronoun** in the sentence below.

My mother sent me an enormous fruit basket, which contained bananas,

grapes, cherries and a mango.

1 mark

38 Complete the sentence below with the **simple past tense** of the verbs in the boxes.

I (to take) _____ my car to a mechanic yesterday to have

it (to repair) _____ but I (to be) _____ not

prepared for the cost!

1 mark

39 Insert a **pair of brackets** in the correct place in the sentence below.

The most populated city in the world is Tokyo population

37,833,000 in Japan.

1 mark

40 Which one **prefix** can be added to all three words below to make their antonyms?

Write the prefix in the box.

decided

forgiving

educated

1 mark

41 Circle the two words that are **synonyms** in the passage below.

The stories written by Roald Dahl are popular with children and adults

around the world. His tales are captivating and yet sometimes a little dark.

1 mark

42 Circle the **possessive pronoun** in the passage below.

I was completely surprised that Sam didn't only eat Amara's ice cream but

ate yours as well.

1 mark

43 Which punctuation mark should be used in the place indicated by the arrow?

My friend moved away last summer his father got a new job in a different city.

Tick **one**.

comma ☐

hyphen ☐

full stop ☐

semi-colon ☐

1 mark

44 Complete each sentence below with a word formed from the **root word** care.

He _____ dropped litter all over the park.

He was always _____ for stray animals he found in the village.

1 mark

45 Complete the sentence below with a noun formed from the **verb** enjoy.

She always found badminton to be a source of great _____.

1 mark

---

46 Insert two **hyphens** in the correct places in the sentence below.

On the way home, I could tell the children were over tired, which they

demonstrated in a very bad tempered way.

1 mark

47 Rewrite the sentence below in the **active** voice.
Remember to punctuate your answer correctly.

The exhausted children were put to bed by the babysitter.

_____

_____ 1 mark

48 Rewrite the underlined verbs in the sentence below so that they are in the
present progressive form.

Judy <u>bakes</u> _____ cakes. She <u>hopes</u> _____

to sell them to her friends on Monday. 1 mark

49 Write a **noun phrase** containing at least three words to complete the
sentence below.
Remember to punctuate your answer correctly.

_____ was working hard in the garden. 1 mark

50 Circle the **adverb** in the sentence below.

You should think hard about your options before making such an

untimely intervention. 1 mark

English grammar, punctuation and spelling

Set B

Paper 2: spelling

Questions and answers

You have approximately **15 minutes** to complete this test.

You will need someone to read the instructions and sentences to you. These can be found in the Contents, Instructions and Answers booklet.

Marks

Each spelling question is worth 1 mark.

Name	
School	

Date of Birth	Day		Month		Year	

Spelling task

1 They played _____ together for hours.

2 I _____ a cold that lasted for a week.

3 Trade with other countries brings jobs and wealth to our _____.

4 It is _____ to me when you are lying.

5 She put a great deal of work into her _____.

6 They found the stories of her adventures quite _____.

7 The new way of organising the paperwork is

quite _____.

8 I know how to dial 999 in the event of an _____.

9 He demonstrated real _____ for the refugees.

10 The sailor looked out at the _____ sea he had ever
encountered.

11 Things were going well until she was scratched

by a _____ in the grass.

12 This is _____ the longest I have ever spent at
my desk.

13 The hotel manager advertised a _____ for
a receptionist.

14 He was a very _____ and patient parent.

15 Something is _____ him, but I'm not sure what it is.

16 I must pop into the _____ for cough medicine on the
way home.

17 My favourite stories are _____ and legends.

18 _____, everyone got on with each other all day.

19 The boys worked all morning on a _____ to the
maths problem.

20 Grandma said she is sending me a _____ for
my birthday.

Key Stage 2 Science Practice Papers
Contents, Instructions and Answers

Author: Thomas Finch

Contents

Biology

Chemistry

Physics

Instructions

Introduction

Matched to the requirements of the national curriculum, this book is designed to help your child practise and prepare for Key Stage 2 tests and assessments.

Administering the Tests

- It contains 9 timed tests, which provide practice of key topics such as living things and their habitats, animals, states of matter, properties of materials, forces, light and electricity.

- The tests are divided into three types: Biology, Chemistry and Physics.

- Each test contains a mixture of question styles to provide the best preparation possible.

- The tests are designed to be completed in 25 minutes. If your child takes more than 25 minutes, then they may need further revision.

Marking the Tests

- Answers are provided on the following pages. Where more than one mark is available, a breakdown of the marks has been provided to show how they should be allocated.

- Using the progress report at the back of the book, your child can instantly see which areas they feel strong in and which areas need further reinforcement.

- After finishing the tests and completing the progress report, your child should revisit the areas where they feel least confident and attempt to improve their score.

Answers

Biology Test 1

Question	Requirement	Mark
1. a		1
1. b	 Stamen — The female part where seeds are made Nectaries — Where nectar is made Petal — The male part where pollen is made Carpel — Attracts insects to the flower Sepals — Protect the flower while it is a bud (0 marks for one correct answer, 1 mark for two or three correct answers, 2 marks for four correct answers, 3 marks for five correct answers)	Up to 3
2. a	Canines – used for tearing and ripping food Incisors – help to bite off bits of food Molars – help to crush and grind food	Up to 3
2. b	Any two from: brush teeth twice a day; avoid sugary food and drinks; visit the dentist regularly	Up to 2
3. a		1
3. b	One of the following for one animal: Giraffe – can consume and store water for long periods of time; long necks to feed and see predators from a distance; tough tongues to pull leaves off without being hurt by thorns Penguin – layer of fat and thick skin to keep warm; huddle together to keep warm; waterproof feathers help them to swim in cold water Camel – long eyelashes to keep sand out of their eyes; nostrils that can open and close; thick eyebrows to shade the eyes from the sun; store fat in their hump Or any other suitable answers.	1
4. a	Any three from: different sizes; different shapes; different colours; different fur; different ears	Up to 3
4. b	Any two from: different eye colour; different hair colour; different feet size; different heights	Up to 2
5. a	 (1 mark for one or two correct answers, 2 marks for three correct answers, 3 marks for four correct answers)	Up to 3
5. b	 Arteries — Tubes that carry blood to the heart Veins — Carries oxygen around the body Blood — Pumps blood around the body Heart — Tubes that carry blood away from the heart (0 marks for one correct answer, 1 mark for two or three correct answers, 2 marks for four correct answers)	Up to 2
6. a	Any two from: to protect important organs in the body; to support the body; to help the body move	Up to 2

6. b	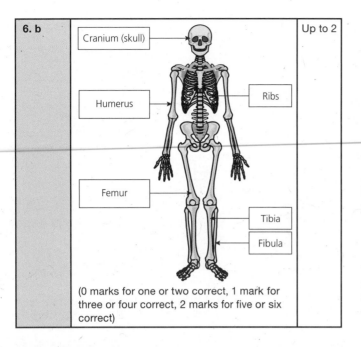	Up to 2

(0 marks for one or two correct, 1 mark for three or four correct, 2 marks for five or six correct)

Labels: Cranium (skull), Humerus, Ribs, Femur, Tibia, Fibula

Biology Test 2

Question	Requirement	Mark
1. a	Any one from: to have a strong stem and keep the plant healthy; so that the plant can make its own food.	1
1. b	Water enters the plant through its roots.	1
1. c	It is transported up the stem to the leaves and flowers.	1
2. a	Glen	1
2. b	Any one from: the smoker will struggle to breathe; the smoker may cough often; the smoker may get lung cancer; any other correct answer.	1
2. c	To help your body and organs work properly.	1
3. a	The heart rate	1
3. b	The children's pulses increase	1
3. c	It is important to increase breathing so more oxygen is moving around the body. Your muscles are working harder so they need more oxygen.	1 1
4. a	cabbage → slug → thrush	1
4. b	Cabbage – Producer Slug – Prey Thrush – Predator	Up to 3
5. a	**3** Excess water is absorbed back into the body in the large intestine. **2** Digested food is absorbed into the bloodstream through the small intestine. **4** Any undigested food passes out when we go to the toilet. **1** Food is eaten, then digested in the mouth, stomach and small intestine.	Up to 2

(0 marks for one correct answer, 1 mark for two correct answers, 2 marks for four correct answers)

5. b	Oesophagus	1
6. a	Any one from: white fur; layer of fat and thick layer of fur; wide large paws	1
6. b	Any one from: white fur helps the polar bear blend in with its surroundings; layers of fat and thick layers of fur keep the polar bear warm; wide paws help the polar bear walk on snow.	1
6. c	1. To see predators in the distance. 2. To reach food that is high in the trees.	1 1
6. d	If the ice is melting it means the polar bears' habitat will slowly disappear, meaning polar bears may disappear one day.	Up to 2

Biology Test 3

Question	Requirement	Mark
1. a	It is missing light	1
1. b	light, water, air	Up to 3
2. a	Any one from: so they are able to stretch more easily; to avoid pulling a muscle when exercising.	1
2. b	When the biceps muscle contracts it will shorten and bring up the lower arm.	Up to 2
3. a	Vertebrates have a backbone but invertebrates do not.	1
3. b		Vertebrate	Invertebrate		Up to 2
		mammals birds	spiders insects		

(1 mark for each correct column)

3. c	Adult → Egg → Chick/hatchling → Adult (life cycle)	1
4. a	**3** Seeds are scattered by an animal or the wind. **1** Pollen is blown by the wind or carried by insects from one plant to another. **2** Pollen reaches the carpel of the new flower and travels to the ovary. It then fertilises ovules to make seed.	Up to 2

(1 mark for one correct answer, 2 marks for three correct answers)

4. b.i	Dispersal	1
4. b.ii	Pollination	1
4. b.iii	Fertilisation	1

4. c	Petal – bright to attract insects Stamen – the male part of the plant that makes the pollen Carpel – the female part of the plant where the seeds are made	Up to 3
4. d	This is when a new plant starts to grow from the seed.	1
4. e	Roots	1
5. a	Grows; eats; cries; urinates; drinks milk (1 mark for one to three correct answers, 2 marks for four or five correct answers)	Up to 2
5. b	(1 mark for one or two correct answers, 2 marks for three or four correct answers)	Up to 2

```
        Foetus
          ↓
Old age        Baby
  ↑             ↓
Adulthood      Child
  ↑             ↓
      Teenager
```

Chemistry Test 1

Question	Requirement	Mark
1. a	Ash, smoke, gases	1
1. b	Irreversible	1
2. a	Rock	1
2. b	3 Rock pushes the sediment down and water washes away the bones, leaving a space in the rock. 5 Fossils are uncovered millions of years later. 2 Sediment falls onto the skeleton of the animal. 1 The animal dies and drops to the river bed. 4 Water carries the rock into the area where the animal was, creating a fossil. (1 mark for one or two correct answers, 2 marks for three correct answers)	Up to 3
2. c	Any two from: how long the animal lived; how things are related; how the animal lived; the environment that they lived in.	Up to 2

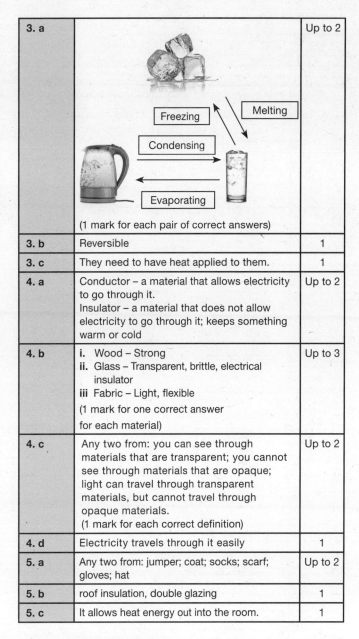

3. a	(1 mark for each pair of correct answers)	Up to 2
3. b	Reversible	1
3. c	They need to have heat applied to them.	1
4. a	Conductor – a material that allows electricity to go through it. Insulator – a material that does not allow electricity to go through it; keeps something warm or cold	Up to 2
4. b	i. Wood – Strong ii. Glass – Transparent, brittle, electrical insulator iii Fabric – Light, flexible (1 mark for one correct answer for each material)	Up to 3
4. c	Any two from: you can see through materials that are transparent; you cannot see through materials that are opaque; light can travel through transparent materials, but cannot travel through opaque materials. (1 mark for each correct definition)	Up to 2
4. d	Electricity travels through it easily	1
5. a	Any two from: jumper; coat; socks; scarf; gloves; hat	Up to 2
5. b	roof insulation, double glazing	1
5. c	It allows heat energy out into the room.	1

Chemistry Test 2

Question	Requirement	Mark
1. a	Hot water	1
1. b	They have dissolved.	1
1. c	She could use hotter water and stir the jelly. This will make the jelly cubes dissolve more quickly.	1 1
2. a	Solids – wood, glass, sand Liquids – water, milk Gases – steam, helium (1 mark for two or three correct answers, 2 marks for four or five correct answers, 3 marks for six or seven correct answers)	Up to 3
2. b	Solids Stays in one place and can be held; keeps its shape; can be cut or shaped Liquids Can flow and be poured; changes shape to fit its container Gases Does not keep its shape; fills the space it is in; can be squashed (1 mark for two correct statements for each state)	Up to 3

3. a	Glass	1
3. b	Glass is the best material for windows because it is transparent	1
3. c	Steel	1
3. d	It means that fabric holds water when it gets wet.	1
3. e	Plastic needs to be heated, then it can be moulded.	1
3. f	Electrical insulator means that electricity cannot pass through a material. Electrical conductor means that electricity can pass through a material.	Up to 2
4. a	1 – Water evaporates into the air. 3 – Water falls as rain. 2 – Water vapour condenses into clouds. 4 – Water returns to the sea. (0 marks for one correct answer, 1 mark for two correct answers, 2 marks for four correct answers)	Up to 2
4. b	The sun heats the water up. This creates water vapour.	1 / 1
4. c	It is changing from vapour to liquid.	1
4. d	1. Lakes 2. Rivers	Up to 2
4. e	Any one from: water evaporates but salt does not; only water evaporates.	1

Chemistry Test 3

Question	Requirement	Mark
1. a	Chalk	1
1. b	Permeable – A permeable rock allows water to soak through it Impermeable – An impermeable rock does not allow water to soak through it.	Up to 2
1. c	Any two from: tiny pieces of rock; tiny pieces of dead plants; tiny pieces of dead animal; tiny pieces of air; tiny drops of water	Up to 2
1. d	B	1
1. e	Funnel 1 – C Funnel 2 – B Funnel 3 – A (1 mark for each correct answer)	Up to 3
2. a	Boiling water – 100°C Warm water – 20°C Water with ice – 5°C Hot water – 50°C (1 mark for one or two correct answers, 2 marks for three or four correct answers)	Up to 2
2. b	The jar containing boiling water.	1
2. c	The water from the melted ice has added to the water that is already in the jar.	1
2. d	It will boil and evaporate	Up to 2
2. e	Condensation	1
2. f	0°C	1
3. a	No because it has been cooked	Up to 2
3. b	Irreversible change	1

3. c	Melting chocolate	1
3. d. i	Heated and melted / Heated and evaporated or Cooled and frozen / Cooled and condensed (1 mark for correct arrows, 1 mark for correct vocabulary, 1 mark for correct order)	Up to 3
3. d. ii	If the ice is heated it will melt into a liquid. If the water is heated the liquid will turn into a gas and evaporate. If the steam is cooled it will condense and turn back into water. If the water is cooled again it will freeze and turn into ice.	Up to 2

Physics Test 1

Question	Requirement	Mark
1. a	Grain of sand – Moon Exercise ball – Sun Tennis ball – Earth	1
1. b	Any one from: every 28 days; every month; every four weeks	1
2. a. i		1
2. a. ii	Yes	1
2. b	No	1
2. c	No	1
2. d	Yes	1
3. a		1
3. b	Natural – one from Sun, candle, oil burner, fire Unnatural – one from electric light, television	Up to 2
4. a	Long grass, carpet, tiles	1
4. b	Eventually the car will stop on all the surfaces because of friction. Friction is caused when two surfaces slide across each other.	Up to 2

5. a			Up to 2
	Magnetic	**Not magnetic**	
	steel iron	gold copper plastic wood	
	(1 mark for each correct column)		
5. b	The magnets will not be attracted to each other because the two north ends are facing each other. The north end needs to face the south end to attract.		Up to 2
5. c	repel		1
6. a	The sound is made through vibrations		1
6. b	higher lower		1
6. c	A soft sound is created by plucking gently on the guitar string. A louder sound is made by plucking the guitar string harder.		1 1

Physics Test 2

Question	Requirement	Mark
1. a	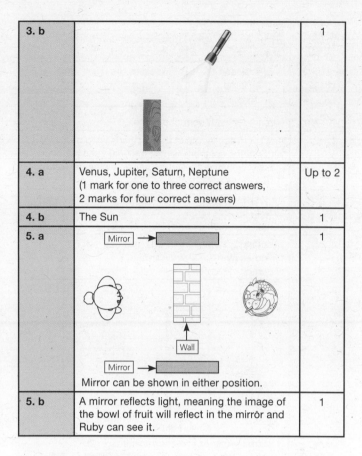 Air resistance Gravity (1 mark for each correct arrow)	Up to 2
1. b	Air resistance – makes the parachute slow down Gravity – pulls the parachute to the ground/ pulls the parachute towards the Earth (1 mark for each correct answer)	Up to 2
1. c	✓	1
1. d	The parachute on the left has a greater surface area, so the air resistance is greater for this parachute.	Up to 2
1. e	The screwed up piece of paper will hit the floor first. It has less surface area than the flat piece of paper.	Up to 2
2. a	Pulley system	1
2. b	Lever system	1
2. c	Gears consist of a system of **cogs** that allows a **small** turning force to have a **great** effect.	Up to 3
3. a	It will increase in length.	1

3. b		1
4. a	Venus, Jupiter, Saturn, Neptune (1 mark for one to three correct answers, 2 marks for four correct answers)	Up to 2
4. b	The Sun	1
5. a	Mirror → Wall Mirror → Mirror can be shown in either position.	1
5. b	A mirror reflects light, meaning the image of the bowl of fruit will reflect in the mirror and Ruby can see it.	1

Physics Test 3

Question	Requirement	Mark
1. a	3. The Earth must orbit the Sun!	1
1. b	The Earth rotates on its axis. When the place you are at is facing the Sun, it is light. When the place you are at is facing away from the Sun, it is dark.	Up to 2
1. c		1
1. d	The Earth rotates on its axis. T It takes the Earth a month to orbit the Sun. F The Moon's full cycle is around 28 days. T One full rotation of the Earth takes a week. F (1 mark for one or two correct answers, 2 marks for three correct answers, 3 marks for four correct answers)	Up to 3
2. a. i	Will work	1
2. a. ii	Will not work	1
2. b	Conductor – a material that will let an electrical current through. Insulator – a material that will not let an electrical current through. (1 mark for each correct answer)	Up to 2

2. c		Up to 2

Runs on electricity	Does not run on electricity
toaster lamp television	coal fire gas hob

(1 mark for each correct column)

3. a	Any two from: length of the spinner's wings; width of the spinner's wings; material used to make the spinner; any other sensible change (1 mark for each change)	Up to 2
3. b	Air resistance Gravity (1 mark for each change)	Up to 2
3. c	Dropping the spinners three times and taking an average improves the accuracy of the test.	1
3. d	 (1 mark for one or two correct answers, 2 marks for three correct answers, 3 marks for four correct answers)	Up to 3
3. e	The one with one paper clip.	1
3. f	As there are no paper clips on the spinner, it will fall more slowly than the spinners that have paper clips on because there is less weight.	1

Biology

- You have 25 minutes to complete this test.

1 Plant structure

a Label the diagram of the plant.

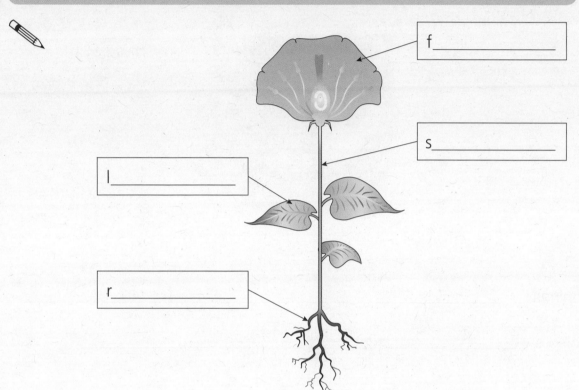

f _____

s _____

l _____

r _____

1 mark

b Draw a line to match each part of the flower with its function.

Stamen	The female part where seeds are made
Nectaries	Where nectar is made
Petal	The male part where pollen is made
Carpel	Attracts insects to the flower
Sepals	Protect the flower while it is a bud

3 marks

2 Teeth

Bob is enjoying his tea. He knows that different teeth have different purposes when eating.

Explain the job of each type of tooth listed below.

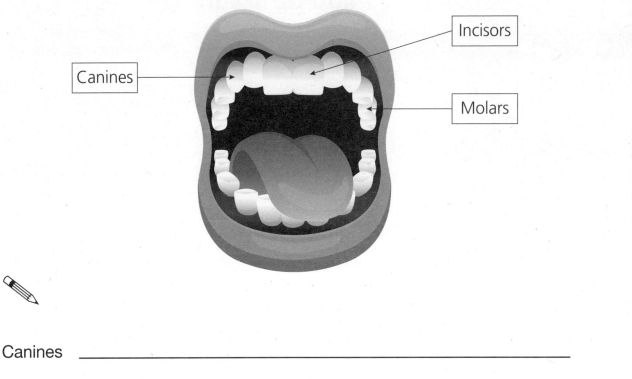

Canines _____

Incisors _____

Molars _____

3 marks

b Bob knows that he needs to keep his teeth healthy.

Suggest **TWO** things Bob must do to keep his teeth healthy.

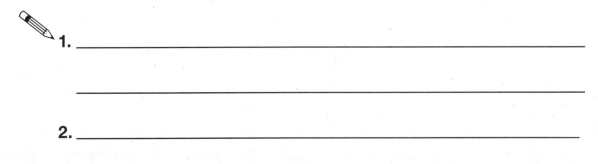

1. _____

_____

2. _____

_____

2 marks

3 Animal adaptations

a Animals have adapted to suit their environments over many years.

Draw a line to match each animal with its environment.

1 mark

b Choose **ONE** of the animals above and give **ONE** way it has adapted to live in its environment.

Animal: _____

How has it adapted? _____

_____ 1 mark

4 Genetics

a This picture shows some dogs.

> Give **THREE** ways in which the dogs show variation.

1. _____

2. _____

3. _____
3 marks

b Children are not usually identical to their parents.

> Name **TWO** ways in which children may not be identical to their parents.

1. _____

2. _____
2 marks

5 The heart

a

Identify the different parts of the circulatory system indicated in the diagram below.

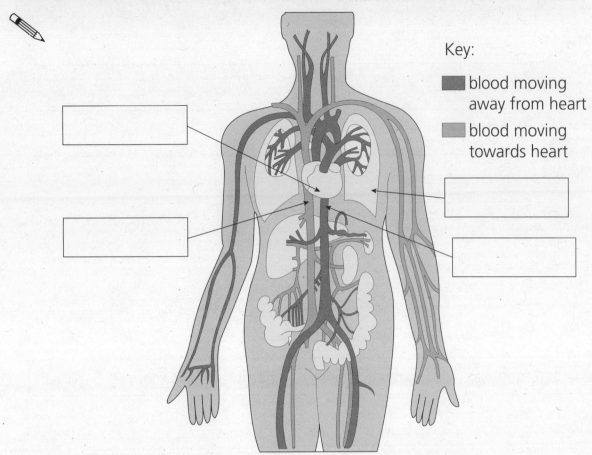

Key:

▮ blood moving away from heart

▮ blood moving towards heart

3 marks

b

Draw a line to match each part of the circulatory system with its function.

Arteries	Tubes that carry blood to the heart
Veins	Carries oxygen around the body
Blood	Pumps blood around the body
Heart	Tubes that carry blood away from the heart

2 marks

6 The human skeleton

a All humans have a bony skeleton.

> Give **TWO** reasons why a skeleton is important.

1. _____

   _____

2. _____

   _____

2 marks

b Use the words in the box below to identify the different parts of the skeleton.

Cranium (skull)   Fibula   Ribs   Femur   Humerus   Tibia

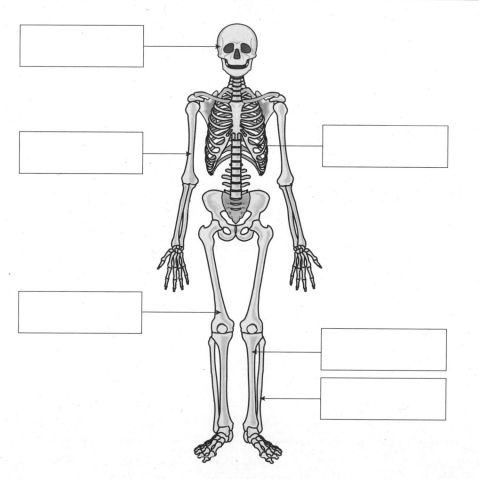

2 marks

Total _____/25 marks

Biology

- You have 25 minutes to complete this test.

1 Plant growth

a Plants need different things to live, including water.

Explain why plants need water.

_____

_____ 1 mark

b Where does water enter the plant?

_____

_____ 1 mark

c How does water get to the leaves and flowers?

_____

_____ 1 mark

2 Healthy lifestyles

a These people answered a survey on their lifestyles.

	Smoker	Healthy diet	Exercise
Ron	Yes	No	No
Kuba	No	Yes	No
Paul	Yes	Yes	Yes
Glen	No	Yes	Yes

Which person has the healthiest lifestyle?

_____

1 mark

b Why is smoking bad for smokers' lungs?

_____

_____

1 mark

c Explain why it is important to have a healthy lifestyle.

_____

_____

1 mark

3 Playing football

a Some children are playing football. Before they start playing, the children measure their pulses.

> What does the pulse measure?

_____
1 mark

b After the children have been playing for 15 minutes, they measure their pulses again.

> What will they notice?

_____
1 mark

c The children need to increase their breathing while doing exercise.

> Why is it important to do this?

_____

_____

_____
2 marks

4 Food chains

a Mia is working on her vegetable patch and has observed the following:

Slugs eat the cabbages.
Thrushes eat the slugs.

Show this on a food chain.

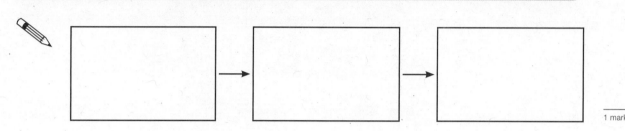

1 mark

b Match the follow things with the correct description.

Cabbage

Prey

Thrush

Producer

Slug

Predator

3 marks

5 Digestion

a The digestive system is important to make sure we get the nutrients we need.

Write a number from 1 to 4 in each box to order these stages in the digestive system from start to finish.

☐ | Excess water is absorbed back into the body in the large intestine.

☐ | Digested food is absorbed into the bloodstream through the small intestine.

☐ | Any undigested food passes out when we go to the toilet.

☐ | Food is eaten, then digested in the mouth, stomach and small intestine.

2 marks

b Tick the name of the tube in which chewed food passes from the mouth to the stomach.

Small intestine ☐

Large intestine ☐

Oesophagus ☐

Rectum ☐

1 mark

6 Animals and their environments

a Animals have changed over millions of years.

> Write down **ONE** feature of a polar bear that helps it in its environment.

_____

1 mark

b How does this help the polar bear in its environment?

_____

_____

1 mark

c Giraffes have developed long necks over time.

> Give **TWO** advantages to the giraffe of having a long neck.

1. _____

_____

_____

2. _____

_____

_____

2 marks

d Over time the polar bears' environment has started to melt away.

> How is this affecting polar bears?

_____

_____

_____

2 marks

Total _____ / 23 marks

Biology

- You have 25 minutes to complete this test.

1 Plants

a Alice is planning an investigation on plants. She has set up three different plants around the room in different places.

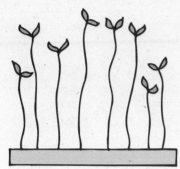  

1. Next to the window   **2.** Inside a cupboard   **3.** Inside a plastic bag in the middle of the room

Alice waters each plant once a day.

> What is plant 2 missing in order to grow well?

_____

_____
1 mark

b Name all **THREE** things that plants need to survive.

1. _____

2. _____

3. _____
3 marks

2 Muscles

a Humans have muscles throughout their bodies.
A group of children are getting ready for a PE lesson.

Why do the children need to warm up and stretch their muscles before exercising?

_____

_____

1 mark

b The biceps muscle in the picture below is currently relaxed.

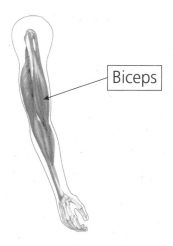

Biceps

Explain what happens when this muscle is contracted.

_____

_____

_____

2 marks

3 Life cycles of animals

a Explain the difference between vertebrate and invertebrate animals.

_____

_____

1 mark

b Sort the following animals into the correct columns in the table.

| Mammals | Birds | Spiders | Insects |

Vertebrate	Invertebrate

2 marks

c Draw the life cycle of a penguin.

1 mark

4 Life cycles of plants

a Plants need to spread their seeds in order to make new plants.

Order the events in this process from 1 to 3.

☐ | Seeds are scattered by an animal or the wind.

☐ | Pollen is blown by the wind or carried by insects from one plant to another.

☐ | Pollen reaches the carpel of the new flower and travels to the ovary. It then fertilises ovules to make seed.

2 marks

b Identify the name of each event in the process.

(i) | Seeds are scattered by an animal or the wind.

_____

1 mark

(ii) | Pollen is blown by the wind or carried by insects from one plant to another.

_____

1 mark

(iii) | Pollen reaches the carpel of the new flower and travels to the ovary. It then fertilises ovules to make seed.

_____

1 mark

c Describe the function of these parts of the plant.

Petal _____

Stamen _____

Carpel _____ 3 marks

d Explain what germination is.

_____

_____

_____ 1 mark

e Tick the part of the plant that takes in water and nutrients.

Leaves ☐

Roots ☐

Stem ☐

Flower ☐

1 mark

5 Human life

a A baby is breathing in his cot.

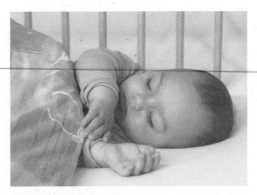

Tick the statements which show the baby is a living thing.

☐	Grows	☐	Drinks milk
☐	Eats	☐	Urinates
☐	Wears a hat	☐	Cries
☐	Sits on the floor	☐	Has a bath

2 marks

b Complete the following life cycle of a human.

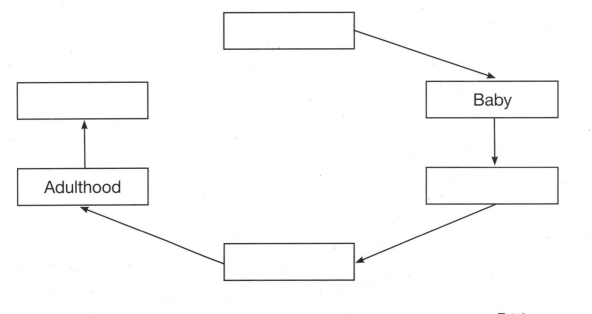

2 marks

Total _____ /25 marks

Chemistry

- You have 25 minutes to complete this test.

1 Fire

a Hashim is making a fire. He lights a match to set fire to the wood.

What **THREE** things are formed when the wood burns?

1. _____

2. _____

3. _____ 1 mark

b What kind of material change is this?

| Irreversible | Reversible | Evaporating | Melting |

_____ 1 mark

2 Fossils

a This is a fossil of an animal from millions of years ago.

What material are fossils made of?

_____

1 mark

b Write a number from 1 to 5 in each box to order the events that took place to make this fossil.

	Rock pushes the sediment down and water washes away the bones, leaving a space in the rock.
	Fossils are uncovered millions of years later.
	Sediment falls onto the skeleton of the animal.
	The animal dies and drops to the river bed.
	Water carries rock into the area where the animal was, creating a fossil.

3 marks

c Scientists can gather information from fossils.

Write down **TWO** things that scientists can learn by examining a fossil.

1. _____

2. _____

2 marks

3 Ice cubes

a Sid is enjoying a cold drink. As he drinks it, the ice cubes begin to melt.

Label each arrow with the name of the change that is happening.

One has been done for you.

| Melting | Evaporating | Freezing | Thawing | Condensing |

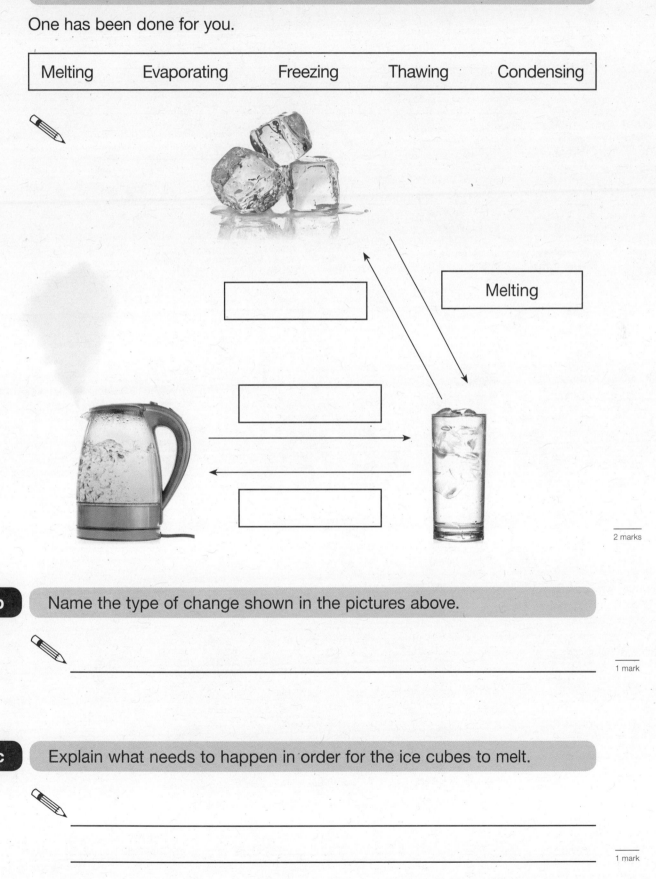

Melting

2 marks

b Name the type of change shown in the pictures above.

_____

1 mark

c Explain what needs to happen in order for the ice cubes to melt.

_____

_____

1 mark

4 Materials

What are the properties of these two materials?

Conductor _____

_____

Insulator _____

_____

2 marks

b Give **ONE** important property of each of the following materials.

(i) Wood

_____

1 mark

(ii) Glass

_____

1 mark

(iii) Fabric

_____
1 mark

c Explain the difference between transparent and opaque.

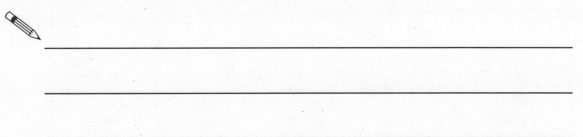

_____

_____

_____
2 marks

d Copper is a good electrical conductor.

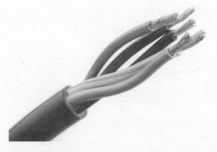

What does it mean if a material has a high value for electrical conductivity?

_____

_____
1 mark

5 Keeping warm

a   Charlotte is trying to keep warm.

Name **TWO** items of clothing she can wear that could keep her insulated.

1. _____

2. _____   2 marks

b   Charlotte wants to improve the length of time her house stays warm.

Which of the following would work? Tick all that apply.

☐   roof insulation

☐   double glazing

☐   wooden roof

☐   single glazing

1 mark

c   A radiator is a thermal conductor.

What does this mean?

_____

_____   1 mark

Total _____/24 marks

Chemistry

- You have 25 minutes to complete this test.

1 Jelly

a Freya is investigating different ways to make jelly.

She is going to make two lots of jelly. First, she dissolves jelly cubes in water. She uses hot water for one lot of jelly cubes and cold water for the other.

> Will the cubes dissolve more quickly in the hot water or the cold water?

_____

1 mark

b Freya notices that the jelly cubes don't look solid anymore.

> What has happened to the jelly cubes in the water?

_____

1 mark

c When making her jelly, Freya wants to speed up the process.

> What could Freya do to speed up the process that happens when she adds the jelly cubes to the water?
> Explain your answer.

_____

_____

_____

2 marks

2 Solids, liquids and gases

Jane is looking at materials. She needs to categorise the materials she is investigating.

Sort the following materials into the correct columns in the table below.

Steam	Water	Wood	Glass	Sand	Helium	Milk

Solids	Liquids	Gases

3 marks

Give **TWO** properties that a material has when it is in each of the states below.

Solid

 1. _____

2. _____

Liquid

 1. _____

2. _____

Gas

 1. _____

2. _____

3 marks

3 New bedroom

Jed is planning a new bedroom. He has a variety of materials to use.

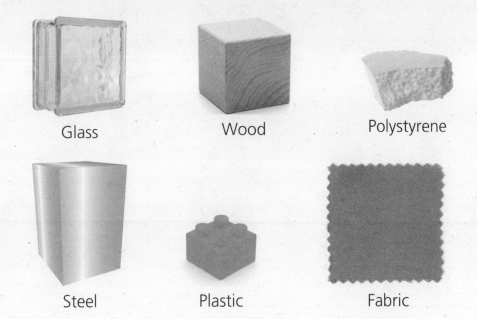

Glass

Wood

Polystyrene

Steel

Plastic

Fabric

Jed needs a material to put into the windows in his room.

Which material would be best to use?

_____

1 mark

b Explain why this is the best material for windows.

_____

_____

1 mark

c Which material is magnetic?

_____

1 mark

d Some fabrics are very absorbent.

What does this mean?

_____

_____
1 mark

e State what would need to be done to plastic to change its shape.

_____

_____
1 mark

f Plastic is a good electrical insulator.

What is the difference between an electrical insulator and an electrical conductor?

Electrical insulator _____

_____

Electrical conductor _____

_____
2 marks

4 Water cycle

The water cycle is an extremely important natural event.

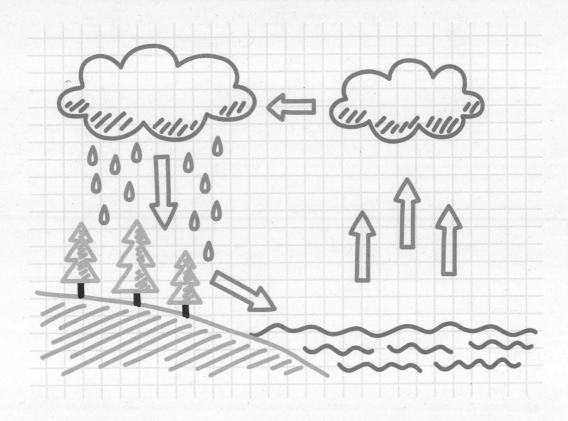

Write a number from 1 to 4 in each box to order these events in the water cycle.

One has been done for you.

| 1 | Water evaporates into the air. |

| | Water falls as rain. |

| | Water vapour condenses into clouds. |

| | Water returns to the sea. |

2 marks

b What makes the water evaporate and what is created?

✏️ _____

_____

_____ 2 marks

c When water vapour condenses, what is happening to the water?

✏️ _____

_____ 1 mark

d Name **TWO** places water collects before it runs back to the sea.

✏️ 1. _____

2. _____ 2 marks

e In the water cycle, salty water from the sea eventually becomes rain water.

Why is rain water not salty?

✏️ _____

_____ 1 mark

Total _____ /25 marks

Chemistry

- You have 25 minutes to complete this test.

1 Rock and soil types

a Kelly has a number of rocks. She tries to scratch each rock with her fingernail. She can scratch off bits of the chalk but she cannot mark the other rocks.

Slate   Marble   Chalk   Granite

Which is the softest rock?

🖉 _____

1 mark

b Kelly pours water onto each rock to see what will happen. Some rocks are permeable and others are impermeable.

What do these terms mean?

Permeable

🖉 _____

_____

_____

Impermeable

🖉 _____

_____

_____

2 marks

c Kelly is planting some plants to grow over the summer. She knows that certain plants will grow better in different soils.

Name **TWO** things that soil is made up of.

1. _____

2. _____   2 marks

d Kelly puts different soils into funnels. She pours the same amount of water into each funnel and observes how much water comes through after 10 minutes.

Water — Soil

A   B   C

Which soil, A, B or C, let the most water through?

_____   1 mark

e Funnel 1: When dry, clay soil has very few air gaps.
Funnel 2: Chalky soil allows water to drain through it quickly.
Funnel 3: When dry, sandy soil has lots of air gaps.

Which funnel has each of the different soils, A, B or C, in it?

Funnel 1 _____

Funnel 2 _____

Funnel 3 _____   3 marks

2 Water temperature

a Jen is given four jars with water in them. She is told that some jars are warmer than others.

> Fill in the table below with Jen's results.

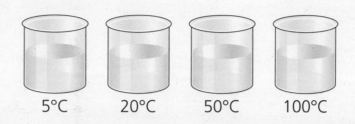

5°C   20°C   50°C   100°C

Jar	Temperature (°C)
Boiling water	
Warm water	
Water with ice	
Hot water	

2 marks

b Jen puts some ice into each of the jars.

> In which jar will the ice melt the fastest?

_____

1 mark

c After the ice has melted Jen notices that the water level has increased from the original amount.

> Why has this happened?

_____

_____

1 mark

d Jen takes the water from one jar and heats it in a pan on a hob.

Explain what will happen to the water.

_____

_____

_____ 2 marks

e What is the name of the process that makes steam change back to liquid water?

_____ 1 mark

f Jen puts another jar of water in the freezer.

At what temperature does water freeze?

_____ 1 mark

3 Changes in materials

a Sarah is making some toast.

Can Sarah turn her toast back into bread? Explain your answer.

✎ _____

_____

2 marks

b What kind of change is this?

✎ _____

1 mark

c Tick which of the following are reversible changes.

✎ Melting chocolate ☐

Baking bread ☐

Frying an egg ☐

1 mark

d The following diagrams are in no particular order.

(i) **Copy** the diagrams and add labelled arrows to show how ice, liquid water and steam are linked by reversible changes.

3 marks

(ii) Explain what your labelled diagram shows.

_____

_____

_____

_____

_____

2 marks

Total _____ / 26 marks

Physics

TEST
1

- You have 25 minutes to complete this test.

1 Earth, Sun and Moon

a Joe is trying to find objects that show the Earth, Moon and Sun to scale for a project.

Write under each object which one of Earth, Moon and Sun would fit best.

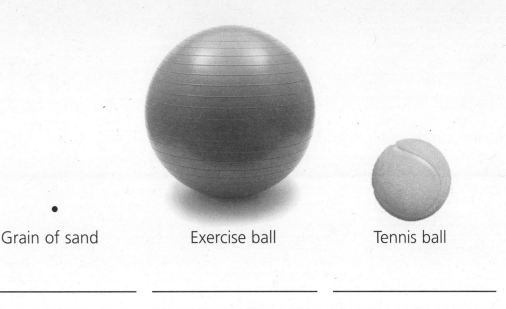

Grain of sand   Exercise ball   Tennis ball

_____   _____   _____

1 mark

b How often does the Moon orbit the Earth?

_____

_____

1 mark

2 Circuits

a Here is part of a series circuit.

(i) Finish drawing the circuit by including a closed switch and a bulb, using the correct symbols.

1 mark

(ii) Will the circuit work?

_____

1 mark

b Will the lamp light in this circuit? Tick the correct answer box.

Yes ☐

No ☐

1 mark

c Will the motor work in this circuit? Tick the correct answer box.

Yes ☐

No ☐

1 mark

d Will the lamps light in this circuit? Tick the correct answer box.

Yes ☐

No ☐

1 mark

3 How we see

a Kamil is exploring how he can see different objects.

Using arrows, show how light travels so Kamil can see his scooter.

1 mark

b Give an example of a natural and an unnatural source of light.

Natural   _____

Unnatural   _____

2 marks

4 Friction

a Isaac has a toy car. He has been exploring how it travels on different surfaces and has noticed that it travels in different ways. He pushes the toy car and lets it go.

> Put the following surfaces in order from the one on which the toy car travels the least distance to the one on which it travels the furthest.

Carpet

Long grass

Tiles

_____
Least

_____

_____
Furthest

1 mark

b Explain why the toy car will eventually stop on the surfaces.

_____

_____

_____

_____

2 marks

5 Magnets

a Sort the following items into magnetic and not magnetic.

| Gold | Steel | Plastic | Iron | Wood | Copper |

Magnetic	Not magnetic

2 marks

b Explain why these magnets will not be attracted to each other.

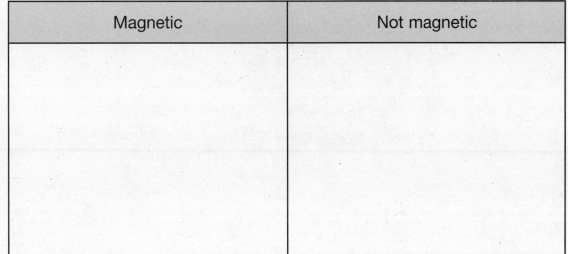

_____

_____

_____

2 marks

c Complete the sentence below.

Sometimes magnets are not attracted to each other. In other words

they _____ each other.

1 mark

6 Making sounds

a Grace plucks the strings on the guitar and hears a sound.

> What makes the sound?

✎ _____

1 mark

b Grace can make sounds of different pitches.

> Complete the following sentences.

✎ Making a string shorter makes a sound with a _____ pitch.

Making a string longer makes a sound with a _____ pitch.

1 mark

c Grace plays a song for her friend.

> Explain how Grace can make a soft sound and a loud sound on her guitar.

✎ _____

_____

_____

_____

2 marks

Total _____ / 22 marks

Physics

- You have 25 minutes to complete the test.

1 Gravity

a Ted drops a parachute from a 5 metre height. He knows that gravity and air resistance are acting on it.

> Draw arrows on the diagram below to show the directions of these two forces.

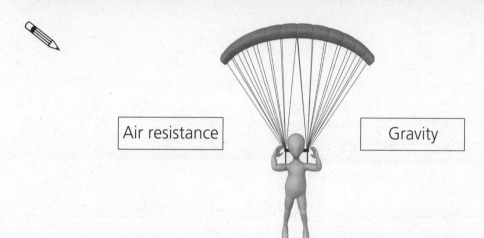

Air resistance   Gravity

2 marks

b Describe how the two forces act on the parachute.

Air resistance

_____

_____

Gravity

_____

_____

2 marks

c Ted has a second parachute. The second parachute is twice the size of the first.

Tick which parachute will fall more slowly.

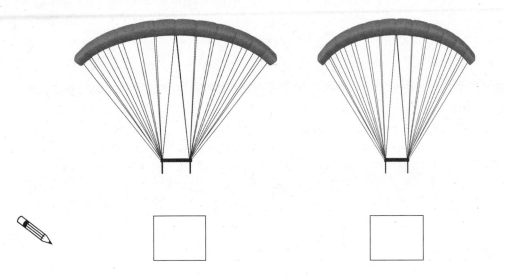

1 mark

d Why does your chosen parachute fall more slowly?
Link your answer to air resistance.

_____

_____

_____

_____

2 marks

e Ted investigates gravity further. He has two pieces of paper. One is screwed up into a ball, the other is flat.

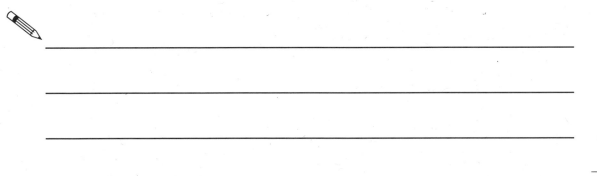

Which piece of paper will hit the floor first when they are dropped at the same time from the same height? Explain your answer.

_____

_____

2 marks

2 Forces

a Jay is collecting water from a well.

> What system is in place to help Jay get the bucket up and down the well?

✏️ _____ — 1 mark

b Name **ONE** other system that can be used to help people against forces.

✏️ _____ — 1 mark

c Complete the following sentence.

✏️ Gears consist of a system of _____ that allows a _____

turning force to have a _____ effect. — 3 marks

---

3 Light and shadows

a Fred has a torch and is investigating how the position of the torch changes the shadow made against a block of wood.

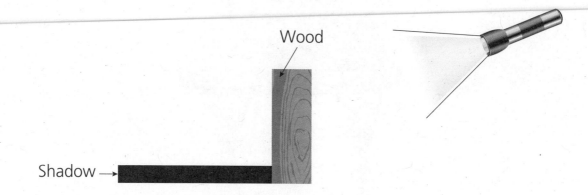

Wood

Shadow →

What will happen to the length of the shadow if the torch is lowered?

_____

_____

1 mark

b Draw where the torch needs to be in order to create a shorter shadow than is shown in the diagram above.

1 mark

4 Planets

a Put these planets in order from the closest to the furthest away from the Sun.

Jupiter

Neptune

Venus

Saturn

_____ _____ _____ _____

Closest   Furthest

2 marks

b Name the star at the centre of our solar system.

_____

1 mark

5 How we see things

a Ruby is trying to look at a bowl of fruit placed behind a wall. She is investigating the ways in which she can see it.

Draw where Ruby could place a mirror in order to see the bowl with the wall in the way.

 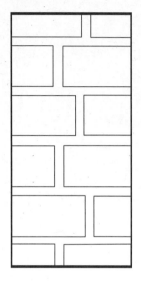 

1 mark

b Explain how Ruby can see the bowl of fruit using a mirror.

_____

_____

_____

1 mark

Total _____ /21 marks

Physics

- You have 25 minutes to complete this test.

1 Day and night

a Kim is making a note of where the Sun is at different times of the day.
She comes up with three reasons for why the Sun moves throughout the day.

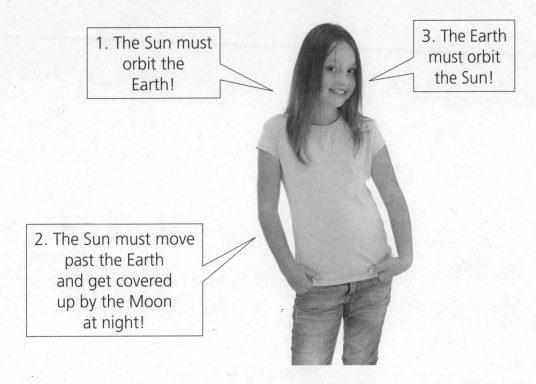

Which of these statements is true?

_____
1 mark

b Explain how day and night occur in more detail.

_____

_____

_____
2 marks

c Kim watches the Moon each night. She notices that the Moon looks different each night and on some nights she can't see it.

On the diagram draw the Moon and how it moves in relation to the Sun and Earth.

1 mark

d Kim comes up with four statements from her investigations on the Sun, Moon and Earth.

Mark if each statement is true (T) or false (F).

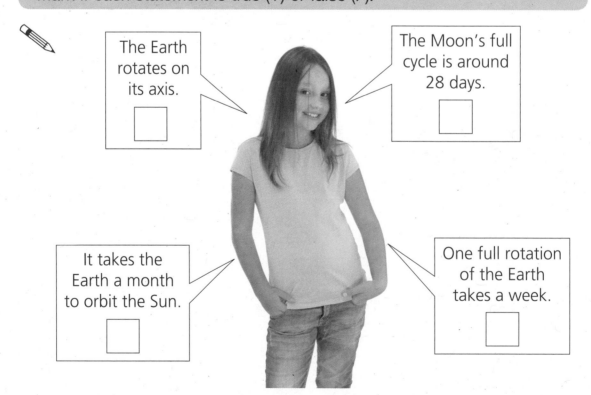

The Earth rotates on its axis.

The Moon's full cycle is around 28 days.

It takes the Earth a month to orbit the Sun.

One full rotation of the Earth takes a week.

3 marks

2 Electrical objects

a Pryia is experimenting with some circuits. She is putting different objects in her circuits to see if the bulb will still light up.

(i) Put a tick in the correct box to indicate if the circuit will or will not work.

Iron bar

Will work ☐

Will not work ☐

1 mark

(ii) Put a tick in the correct box to indicate if the circuit will or will not work.

Plastic tube

Will work ☐

Will not work ☐

1 mark

b Pryia knows that there are electrical conductors and electrical insulators.

Explain what each of these are.

Conductor

_____

_____

Insulator

_____

_____

2 marks

c Pryia looks at some objects around her house. She organises them into two categories: runs on electricity and does not run on electricity.

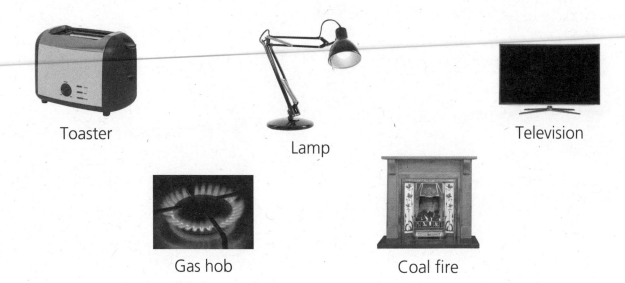

Toaster

Lamp

Television

Gas hob

Coal fire

Sort the items into these two categories.

Runs on electricity	Does not run on electricity

2 marks

3 Spinners

a Katie is preparing her spinners for an investigation into forces. She is trying to think of something that she can change in her experiment. She decides to change the number of paper clips attached to the bottom of the spinner before she drops it.

> Write down **TWO** other changes she could have made.

1. _____

2. _____   2 marks

b Katie performs the investigation and drops each spinner from the same height.

> Which **TWO** main forces are acting on the spinner as it drops?

1. _____

2. _____   2 marks

c Katie creates a table to show her results.

Number of paper clips	Time (s)
1	5.0
2	4.1
3	2.9
4	2.5

Katie dropped each spinner three times. She then took an average of the results.

> Why does Katie need to drop each spinner three times and take an average?

_____

_____   1 mark

d Katie then creates a bar chart showing her results. Complete the bar chart.

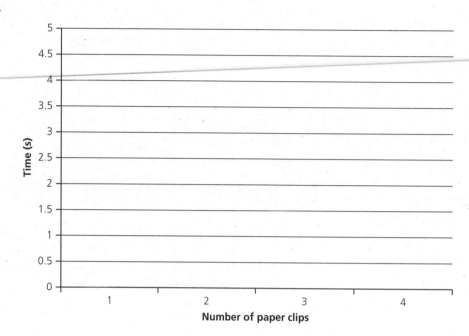

Time (s)

5
4.5
4
3.5
3
2.5
2
1.5
1
0.5
0

1   2   3   4

Number of paper clips

3 marks

e Katie uses her graph to interpret the results.

Which spinner fell the slowest?

1 mark

f Explain what would happen if there was a spinner with no paper clips.

1 mark

Total _____ /23 marks

Progress Report

Fill in your total marks for each completed test.

Colour the stars to show how you feel after completing each test.

☆ = needs practice   ☆☆ = nearly there   ☆☆☆ = got it!

Biology

Test	Marks	How do you feel?
Test 1	/ 25	☆ ☆ ☆
Test 2	/ 23	☆ ☆ ☆
Test 3	/ 25	☆ ☆ ☆

Chemistry

Test	Marks	How do you feel?
Test 1	/ 24	☆ ☆ ☆
Test 2	/ 25	☆ ☆ ☆
Test 3	/ 26	☆ ☆ ☆

Physics

Test	Marks	How do you feel?
Test 1	/ 22	☆ ☆ ☆
Test 2	/ 21	☆ ☆ ☆
Test 3	/ 23	☆ ☆ ☆

Acknowledgements

The authors and publisher are grateful to the copyright holders for permission to use quoted materials and images.

English Reading booklet Set A: P23 © Douglas Carr/Alamy Stock Photo; P24 ©Granger Historical Picture Archive/Alamy Stock Photo

All other illustrations ©Shutterstock.com and © HarperCollins*Publishers*

Every effort has been made to trace copyright holders and obtain their permission for the use of copyright material. The authors and publisher will gladly receive information enabling them to rectify any error or omission in subsequent editions. All facts are correct at time of going to press.

Published by Collins
An imprint of HarperCollins*Publishers*
1 London Bridge Street
London SE1 9GF

HarperCollins*Publishers*
Macken House, 39/40 Mayor Street Upper,
Dublin 1 Ireland D01 C9W8

© HarperCollins*Publishers* Limited 2018

ISBN 9780008384548

Content first published 2018
This edition published 2020

10

British Library Cataloguing in Publication Data.

A CIP record of this book is available from the British Library.

Authors: Faisal Nasim and Thomas Finch
Contributors: Tom Hall and Jon Goulding
Commissioning Editors: Michelle l'Anson,
Alison James, Chantal Addy and Fiona McGlade
Editorial: Katie Galloway, Lesley Montford and Richard Toms
Cover Design: Kevin Robbins and Sarah Duxbury
Inside Concept Design: Paul Oates and Ian Wrigley
Text Design and Layout: Aptara® Inc
Production: Lyndsey Rogers
Printed in India by Multivista Global Pvt. Ltd

MIX
Paper | Supporting responsible forestry
FSC www.fsc.org
FSC™ C007454

This book is produced from independently certified FSC™ paper to ensure responsible forest management.

For more information visit:
www.harpercollins.co.uk/green